Education of Syrian Refugee Children

Managing the Crisis in Turkey, Lebanon, and Jordan

Shelly Culbertson, Louay Constant

For more information on this publication, visit www.rand.org/t/RR859

Library of Congress Cataloging-in-Publication Data is available for this publication.
ISBN: 978-0-8330-9239-7

Published by the RAND Corporation, Santa Monica, Calif.

© Copyright 2015 RAND Corporation

RAND® is a registered trademark.

Cover image: Syrian children in a school in Jordan (Shelly Culbertson).

www.rand.org

Preface

The Syrian civil war has displaced half of Syria's population, with civilians fleeing internally or to other countries. Neighboring countries—particularly Lebanon, Turkey, Jordan, Iraq, and Egypt—have generously opened borders to the refugees in response to such great humanitarian need, and the international aid community has responded with assistance. The Syrian refugee crisis is now spilling over into Europe. A particular area of concern is education for the refugee children, important for the future of Syrian and host country societies. This scoping study is intended to contribute to the ongoing policy discussions among governments, donors, and United Nations agencies about the education of Syrian refugees in Lebanon, Turkey, and Jordan (the three countries with the largest populations of Syrian refugees), on four topics:

- **Access:** How can refugee children access education?
- **Management:** How will refugee education be planned, managed, and supported?
- **Society:** How can refugee education promote a stable and prosperous society? How can plans for refugee education be managed within sensitive political constraints?
- **Quality:** How can the quality of education for both refugees and host country citizens be promoted in such difficult circumstances?

The report concludes with policy implications, discussions of trade-offs among goals within resources and political constraints, and needed areas of further research.

The Center for Middle East Public Policy

This research was supported through philanthropic contributions and conducted under RAND's Initiative for Middle East Youth (IMEY) within the RAND Center for Middle East Public Policy (CMEPP), part of International Programs at the RAND Corporation. The RAND Corporation is a nonprofit institution that helps improve policy and decisionmaking through research and analysis. RAND focuses on the issues that matter most, such as education, health, national security, international affairs, law and business, the environment, and more. CMEPP brings together analytic excellence and regional expertise from across the RAND Corporation to address the most critical political, social, and economic challenges facing the Middle East today. For more information about the RAND Center for Middle East Public Policy, visit www.rand.org/cmepp or contact the director (contact information is provided on the web page).

Contents

Figures and Tables

Summary

The Syrian refugee situation is one of the most devastating humanitarian crises of our time. From the start of the civil war in 2011 to September 2015, half of Syria's population of 23 million has been displaced, with at least 7.6 million displaced internally and 4 million refugees. The influx of the Syrian refugees is on such a large scale that it is altering the demographics of countries that have accepted them, increasing Lebanon's population by more than 25 percent, Jordan's population by 10 percent, and the population of border areas of Turkey by 10–20 percent. The governments and citizens of these countries have demonstrated remarkable generosity toward the refugees.

But the presence of the refugees has placed significant demands on overstretched public service sectors and has caused tensions in countries that face their own development and stability challenges. It has caused crowding in schools and hospitals; rents have risen in poorer areas; and there are downward pressures on wages or worsening unemployment in economies that already have high unemployment. Public sectors lack needed resources, and educational, health, and other services cannot keep pace. Government budgets and infrastructure are increasingly burdened, and funding from the international community does not cover the costs. In communities that are most affected by a significant refugee presence, direct tensions can arise between host country nationals and Syrians, causing concerns for security and social cohesion.

While the refugees, governments, and host country citizens would all prefer that the refugees could return to their homes soon, children who have missed several years of education, and an approach to certification.

Create additional shifts in public schools, with greater attention to quality. Shifts could provide fast additional space for government or alternative formal education. Adding school days could compensate for shortened instructional time that comes with shifting schools.

Analyze scope of barriers to access, and develop plans to address them. Compare the importance of reasons that children are out of school and develop plans to solve the problems.

Pursue an innovative school financing and building plan. A school building strategy should include (1) facilitation of both short- and longer-term scenarios (to the extent possible), (2) repurposing of buildings, (3) building additional schools, (4) innovative financing, and (5) global and regional longer-term funding commitments.

Management Policy Considerations

Host governments, UN agencies, NGOs, donors, and refugees themselves are involved in education provision; school facilities and supplies; teacher supply and training; monitoring, oversight, and information; overarching policy-setting and resourcing; and supporting functions. Establishing education for such large numbers of refugees is a complex management task that requires short-term solutions, long-term planning, and evidence upon which to base decisions. We suggest the following in support of management of refugee education.

Include longer-term development planning in addition to humanitarian responses. To date, much of the refugee response has been responding to the emergency, focusing on short-term solutions. Given that it is more than four years into the crisis, planning should move to a longer-term development response involving greater resourcing and capacity-building of national education ministries (or alternative systems with quality standards and monitoring), to leave countries with a system that can be managed over time.

Prioritize funding to support formal education. As funding is limited and likely to decline further in the future, it should be prioritized with longer-term donor commitments to support formal education, as opposed to the current range of short-term supportive programs.

Invest in building capacity for governments to manage the crisis into the future. Governments need improved management systems to support increased responsibilities, with respect to refugee education.

Enhance data and information in support of managing refugee education. Information about education is lacking to support decisionmaking and planning. Information may be improved by collecting data about key questions, developing a consistent set of indicators, building capacity of government data management, and enabling multiple actors to contribute to data systems.

Improve effectiveness and efficiency of the refugee education response with creative use of technology. Mobile phones, data systems, the Internet, and YouTube all present opportunities.

Society Policy Considerations

The existence of so many refugees, to the extent that their numbers change national demographics, presents significant challenges to Syrian and host-country society and well-being. Several of these societal challenges are related to education, including how children are integrated in school, certification of education to provide pathways to the labor market or further education, the need to improve livelihoods to reduce child labor or early marriage and enable education, and how schools and teachers manage the psychosocial needs of children. The size of the Syrian refugee population in relation to host societies complicates delicate intergroup balances. We offer several approaches.

Weigh the advantages and disadvantages of integration or separation of the Syrians within public schools, and create a deliberative strategy to address this question. There are compelling reasons that many Syrians are separated from citizens in the classroom in the short term: They are being taught in second shifts, Syrian community schools, or schools run by UN agencies. However, in the long term, this risks creating a population that is separated from the rest of the community (like the Palestinian refugees), with a perception of receiving lower-quality services, lack of labor market opportunities, and reduced opportunities for higher education.

Coordinate curriculum standards and certification exams on a regional level as a strategy to prepare Syrian students for two scenarios: returning to life in Syria and integrating into the host countries. We suggest a comparison of the curriculum standards of Syria with that of Turkey, Jordan, Lebanon, and the Syrian Adapted Curriculum (associated with the Syrian opposition). We also advise looking into development of options for Syrians to obtain certification in both the host country system and Syrian system, as well as creation of a program administered by an international organization to enable Syrian students to take exams in both host counties and Syria.

Develop a plan to enable Syrian employment, with consideration for mitigating the effects on the local labor markets. A lack of ability for Syrians to work and support their families creates circumstances that drive down host-country wages and promote Syrian refugee child labor and early marriage, precluding school attendance. We suggest a labor market study and development of an evidence-based approach to balance host-country economic considerations with the need for Syrians' livelihoods. Syrian employment also could enable collecting taxes, which could be used to support public services such as education.

Develop programs at the national scale to better prepare schools and teachers to address the psychosocial needs of refugee students. Schools need structured programs to meet the psychosocial needs of students, and teachers need training in dealing with the needs particular to a refugee population.

Quality Policy Considerations

Host governments, UN agencies, NGOs, and the refugee community are striving to provide education to refugee children. However, accommodating the education needs of so many has posed challenges to the quality of education, for both refugees and citizens, as resources are strained and public education systems struggle to keep up. Several steps could mitigate these challenges.

Ensure adequate instructional time in first- and second-shift schools by adding school days. To create more school spaces, Lebanon and Jordan have created second shifts for Syrians in public schools. Studies of countries such as South Korea and Brazil suggest that students in double-shift schools can perform as well as students in single-shift schools, provided that there is enough instructional time and the shifts are equally resourced.

Strategically support teachers with refugees in their classrooms. This could include additional training for host-country teachers, mixing experienced teachers and new hires in the same schools and shifts, and when appropriate, incorporating Syrian refugees who worked as teachers.

Introduce new schools and shifts into national school monitoring systems, and develop additional monitoring and support approaches appropriate to the new situations. In all three countries, additional school monitoring and support for the schools or shifts for the Syrian students is needed. This may mean integration into existing national school monitoring programs, developing new modes of training and quality monitoring specific to needs of refugee children, and development of quality frameworks and monitoring for alternative formal education programs.

Keep focused attention on the education needs of host-country nationals. Amid all of this, the needs of host-country nationals should be prioritized, planned, financed, and addressed.

Final Considerations and Trade-Offs

Clearly, managing refugee education and implementing new initiatives is no easy task, particularly for such a large population that grew quickly. While this study serves as a broad overview of the circumstances, challenges, and ideas for the way forward, further studies are needed to assess feasibility, optimal options, and implementation. To provide additional perspectives on the policy considerations presented in this report, we propose a set of goals and considerations to guide further planning, based on interviews, literature review, and analysis. While education stakeholders might debate some of these goals and how to prioritize them, these goals as a group are contributing both their explicit and tacit assumptions underlying the Syrian refugee education response. Goals include cost-effectiveness, using existing resources, managing different future scenarios, host-community relations, equity, shared responsibility, political feasibility, government capacity, speed, benefits to host countries, quality and values, safety, sustainability, cohesive national identities, native language education, host country language proficiency, no long-term parallel education system, integration, decisiveness and speed, and deliberative strategies.

These goals are ambitious. A significant risk in moving forward is that many of these goals conflict with each other. Trade-offs will have to be made. We argue that the foremost goal is wider access, particularly addressing the formal education needs of the 542,000 Syrian refugee children out of school in Lebanon, Turkey, and Jordan.

Acknowledgments

The authors would like to thank the following stakeholders for participating in interviews, sharing documents and data, and contributing ideas. We are grateful to Jordan's Ministry of Education, Jordan's Ministry of Planning and International Cooperation, the Office of King Abdullah in Jordan, Lebanon's Ministry of Education and Higher Education, the U.S Agency for International Development (USAID), the U.S. State Department (Population, Migration, and Refugees), UNICEF, UNESCO, UNHCR, UNDP, International Organization for Migration, Save the Children, Catholic Relief Services, Caritas, Jordan University's Center for Strategic Studies, ACTED, and Heritage College in Lebanon. (We note that not all United Nations agencies and nongovernmental organizations were interviewed in each country.)

We also would like to thank CMEPP board member William Recker for his generous time and support for this project, as well as the other CMEPP board members whose philanthropic contributions make these types of studies possible.

We would like to thank the members of the project Senior Advisory Board for their advice and constructive feedback: Dalia Dassa-Kaye, Darleen Opfer, Charles Ries, and Robin Meili for their guidance and support throughout this project. We thank James Hoobler, Semira Ahdiyyih, and Katya Migacheva for their contributions to the literature review, and Michelle Horner for document support.

Finally, we would like to thank Robin Meili (director of International Programs at RAND) for our RAND quality assurance review. We thank Rita Karam (policy researcher at RAND and professor at the Pardee RAND Graduate School), Elizabeth Ferris (codirector of the Brookings-London School of Economics Project on Internal Displacement), and Musa Shteiwi (director of the Center for Strategic Studies at the University of Jordan) for their peer reviews of the report.

CHAPTER ONE

Introduction

Background and Study Objectives

There are more people displaced by conflict in the world now than at any point since World War II (United Nations High Commissioner for Refugees [UNHCR], 2015c). As of the end of 2014, there were 60 million people displaced by conflict internationally. Twenty million of these are refugees who have crossed state borders; 38 million are internally displaced persons (IDPs) who are displaced within their own countries; and two million are asylum seekers. Half of these displaced people are children (UNHCR, 2014d). Displacement for many is not short-term but rather becomes a long-term way of life; the average duration of refugee situations is 17 years (Executive Committee of the High Commissioner's Programme, 2004).

The Syrian civil war has created one of the largest and most complex humanitarian crises of our time. Since the start of the civil war in 2011 to September 2015, half of Syria's population of 23 million has been displaced, with at least 7.6 million displaced internally and 4 million refugees (UNHCR, 2015a; UNHCR, 2015d). This makes the Syrian refugees the second-largest refugee population in the world, after the nearly five million Palestinian refugees (Nebehay, 2015).

The Syrian civil war has also created an education crisis for the Middle East. The UNHCR estimates that fewer than half of Syrian refugee children are enrolled in formal education (Regional Refugee and Resilience Plan [3RP], 2015b). A generation of Syrian children is at risk of missing a formal education. Many children have been out of school for years, as schooling in Syria was interrupted and educational systems in host countries have not been able to accommodate all of the refugees (United Nations Children's Fund [UNICEF], 2014a). The futures of individual Syrian children, as well as the stability and prosperity of the region, will depend on ensuring that school-age children receive the education they need to be resilient to the circumstances they face and to develop the capability to provide for themselves and their families. Lacking the protective environment of education, development of critical thinking skills, and the opportunities that result from education also could make more youth vulnerable to recruitment to radical groups. Reports with provocative titles illustrate the risks: *Shattered Lives: Challenges and Priorities for Syrian Children and Women in Jordan, No Lost Generation: Protecting the Futures of Children Affected by the Crisis in Syria,* and *The Future of Syria: Refugee Children in Crisis.* (UNICEF, 2013a; UNICEF, 2014a; UNHCR, 2013).

Given the numbers of Syrian refugee children who are not receiving any formal education, the limited capacities of host countries, the political balances, and the risks that these elements pose to the children and wider society, there is need to alleviate the situation with innovative educational strategies to coordinate efforts, share knowledge, make evidence-based decisions, improve efficiency or effectiveness, and solicit resources.

This scoping study, funded by RAND's Center for Middle East Public Policy, provides an overview of education of Syrian refugees in Lebanon, Turkey, and Jordan (the three countries that have absorbed the largest numbers of Syrian refugees), describes complexities and trade-offs, and offers practical recommendations.

Regional Context and Considerations

Syrian refugees have mainly fled to neighboring countries of Lebanon, Turkey, Jordan, Iraq, and Egypt. The influxes of Syrian refugees are at such a scale that they are altering the demographics of countries that have accepted them. Figure 1.1 illustrates the demographic changes from the Syrian refugee crisis in Lebanon, Turkey, and Jordan as of September 2015.

Figure 1.1
The Scale of the Syrian Refugee Crisis in Lebanon, Turkey, and Jordan

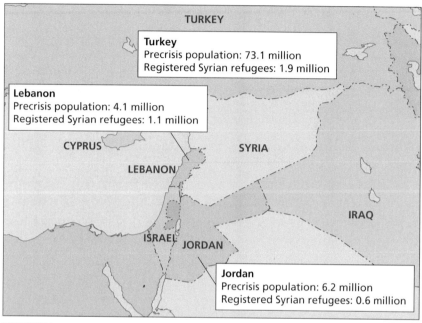

TURKEY

Turkey
Precrisis population: 73.1 million
Registered Syrian refugees: 1.9 million

Lebanon
Precrisis population: 4.1 million
Registered Syrian refugees: 1.1 million

CYPRUS   SYRIA

LEBANON

IRAQ

ISRAEL   JORDAN

Jordan
Precrisis population: 6.2 million
Registered Syrian refugees: 0.6 million

RAND RR859-1.1

Lebanon and Jordan now have the highest per capita ratio of refugees in the world (3RP, 2015c). Before the crisis in 2011, Jordan's population was 6.2 million; the arrival of 630,000 registered refugees means that at least 10 percent of the population of Jordan is now Syrian refugees (UNHCR, 2015d; World Bank, 2015); the Jordanian government puts the total number, including non-registered refugees, as high as 1.4 million (Ministry of Planning and International Cooperation [MOPIC], 2015). Approximately 1.1 million Syrian refugees are registered in Lebanon. With a precrisis population of 4.4 million, this means that refugees increased Lebanon's population by more than 25 percent in a span of a few years. There are 1.9 million Syrian refugees registered with the UNHCR in Turkey, compared with Turkey's precrisis population of 73.1 million. In Turkey's southeast, where the bulk of the refugees have located, refugees are estimated to compose 10–20 percent of the population in some places (Idiz, 2014; Gaziantep

City, undated; Albayrak, 2014). In addition, 250,000 Syrian refugees have registered in Iraq, and 130,000 have registered in Egypt. Interviewees for this study note that these figures represent only registered refugees and estimate that actual numbers (including unregistered refugees) are much higher.

A contributing factor to the challenges in addressing the refugee crisis has been how quickly the numbers of refugees have grown. In June 2012, there were 78,000 refugees. By October 2015, there were 4 million refugees. Figure 1.2 shows the growth in the number of Syrian refugees, from June 2012 through October 2015 (United Nations Office for the Coordination of Humanitarian Affairs (OCHA), 2012, 2013a, 2013b, 2014a, 2014b, 2015).

The three neighboring countries in this study have generously accepted, supported, and provided public-sector services to Syrian refugees, taking on great expense in doing so. By the end of 2014, Turkey had spent $4.5 billion on the refugee response (Anadolu Agency, 2014), the government of Jordan took a $150 million loan to cover additional

Figure 1.2
Growth in Syrian Refugees, June 2012 to October 2015

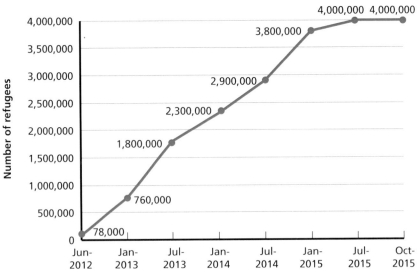

costs of refugee education and health for 2014 (Yukhananov, 2013), and Jordanian officials announced that the government there has been covering over 80 percent of the costs associated with the refugee crisis with the international community covering the remainder (Alvdalat, 2015). In Lebanon in 2013, the ratio of the budget deficit to gross domestic profit rose significantly for the first time since 2006, exceeding 140 percent (Kasbar, 2014). Even before Syria's civil war, Lebanon, Jordan, and Turkey faced their own economic, security, and development problems, now heightened by the wars on their borders and the influx of refugees in need of basic services. Turkey has greater resources than the other countries, which also means that they receive less assistance. Conditions for the refugees in the neighboring countries have become so strained that the refugee crisis is now spilling into Europe.

The Syrian refugee crisis is largely an urban crisis in all three countries. More than 84 percent of Syrian refugees in Jordan are living outside of the camps in communities (UNHCR, 2014h; MOPIC, 2014b). Similarly, in Turkey in December 2014, fewer than 15 percent of registered refugees were in 22 camps; the remaining 85 percent were in host communities—and given that many refugees are not registered, the proportion in host communities may be much higher (UNHCR, 2015b). Unlike in Turkey and Jordan, the government of Lebanon has made a decision to not open formal, serviced refugee camps; refugees either live in host communities or in informal tented settlements. In all three countries, refugees outside of camps are staying with relatives and friends, renting shared accommodations for several families, setting up impromptu makeshift settlements, squatting in abandoned buildings, and finding other solutions for ways to live.

Hosting refugees in urban areas or host communities rather than camps presents both opportunities and constraints. In 2009, UNHCR began encouraging hosting refugees in urban areas rather than camps (UNHCR, 2009). Living in urban areas may be better for the longer-term integration, livelihood, self-reliance, and dignity of refugees, as well as the capacities of the countries to absorb new residents. On the other hand, it also presents challenges to the most-vulnerable refugees, as well to as the international community in reaching them. There is more control and accountability of such services as education when refugees are in camps, because humanitarian actors can locate them easily—a more difficult task when refugees are dispersed in host communities. In addition, when refugees are in camps, their presence is less visible to host-country citizens (who might harbor greater resentment against refugees living in host communities).

Furthermore, while there are differences in financial and management capacity across the three countries' governments, there is crowding in schools and hospitals; rents have risen in poorer areas; and there are downward pressures on wages or increasing unemployment in economies that already have high jobless rates. Public sectors lack needed resources and educational, health, and other services cannot keep pace. Government budgets and infrastructure are increasingly burdened, and funding from the international community does not cover the costs (Olwan, 2009; Davis and Taylor, 2013; Harvard Field Study Group, 2014). By June 2015, less than a quarter of the United Nations' (UN's) $4.5 billion funding request for the Syrian refugees had been given by donors (3RP, 2015a). In communities most affected by a significant refugee presence, it can lead to direct tensions between host-country nationals and Syrians, causing concerns for security and social cohesion. The crisis has also hurt economies because it has diminished cross-border trade with Syria. One interviewee in Turkey said "the whole system is overwhelmed" by the ongoing refugee crisis.

Time Frames, Scenarios, and the Politics of Expectations

There are many incentives to view the Syrian refugee crisis as temporary: Hosting refugees requires significant resources, refugees want to go home, and citizens fear the demographic changes that refugees bring. There is a delicate balance among managing political pressures of having so many refugees competing with citizens for public services, housing, and employment; humanitarian responses for refugees; development needs of countries to invest in their own citizens; and security needs of hosting a new group of traumatized, potentially politically mobilized people. (Orhan, 2014; Dinçer et al., 2013; Cagaptay and Menekse, 2014; Black, 2014; International Labour Organization [ILO], 2014; Naylor, 2015).

But the war does not appear close to resolution. And even if there is a political settlement in Syria, many Syrian refugees likely will not go home for many years because of residual societal tensions, infrastructure destruction, and the weakened economy (Jenkins, 2014). Many refugees have little to return to: In a survey of refugees in Turkey, half said that their homes were either completely destroyed or very damaged (Disaster and Emergency Management Presidency [AFAD], 2013). Furthermore, protracted refugee situations around the world historically show that they are not resolved quickly; as stated above, it takes an average of 17 years before refugees can return to their home countries (Loescher and Milner, 2009). This is not the first time these countries have hosted refugees: Other waves of refugees have included the Palestinians from the Arab-Israeli conflicts in 1948 and 1967, Iraqis from the Iraq war, and European and Central Asian Muslims who fled to Turkey after the redrawing of national borders resulting from the fall of the Ottoman Empire. Many of those refugees stayed permanently, shaping the modern Middle East. Therefore, the presence of the Syrians in neighboring countries is likely to be a medium- to long-term situation.

There are substantial political sensitivities around questions of how long the Syrian refugees will stay, and whether the refugee response should be based on assumptions of a short-term stay, a longer-term stay, or permanence. While it is likely that many refugees will remain for the coming years, governments face pressures to not recognize this publicly and to make plans based on assumptions of a short-term presence (Orhan, 2014; Dinçer et al., 2013; Cagaptay and Menekse, 2014; Black, 2014; ILO, 2014; Naylor, 2015). Many citizens want the refugees to be there temporarily and then to return to Syria. Host governments have reason for not wanting to take measures to support local integration of the Syrian refugees or to acknowledge the potential long-term nature of the demographic changes, as happened with the Palestinian refugees over recent decades. Lebanon's delicate sectarian balance among Sunnis, Shiites, Christians, and Druze would face disruption by the Syrian, mostly Sunni, refugees. Similarly, in Jordan, Palestinian refugees and their descendants now make up half of Jordan's population. Citizens in Lebanon, Jordan, and Turkey have accommodated the refugees under the assumption that their presence would be temporary.

All these sensitivities and pressures add up to political obstacles to implementing plans that appear to be based on the premise that the Syrians will be a long-term presence. But there is still need for longer-term thinking. This tension of addressing short-term needs, a longer-term reality, and the politics of expectations for the refugees has been a feature of many other refugee crises and has never been resolved easily. Many of these displacements lack solutions to this day (Ferris, Kirişci, and Shaikh, 2013). The Middle East, in particular, risks becoming a region of long-term displacement without longer-term integrated solutions.

Education is inextricably tied up with the politics of how long the Syrians will remain in these countries. While governments may not be able to publicly acknowledge the possible long-term nature of this crisis, they still will need plans that would enable them to manage multiple scenarios of the Syrians' presence, for both the short and long term. At the same time, in terms of human rights, the future of Syrian society, and national security, it is important to adopt policies that enable a minimum standard of living for the Syrians. Public services, including education, will need to be provided, without necessarily resting on the assumption that the refugees will be a long-term presence (or precluding their eventual departure). Yet, there has been little long-term development planning to help these governments create the infrastructure and policies to manage refugee education for the coming decades. Until very recently, the refugee education response was addressed as a short-term effort with temporary programs. Like the refugees, governments and UN agencies were planning as if this crisis would be over soon.

Given the importance of such public services as education, as well as the uncertainties and complexities about the future of the Syrian refugees in these countries, there is need to conduct analysis in the spirit of "scenario planning," initially developed at the RAND Corporation after World War II and now used widely in government and business planning (Chermack, Lynham, and Ruona, 2001). In scenario planning, alternative futures are mapped out, and the plans that best meet the diverse needs of multiple alternative futures are adopted. In this case, while it is beyond the scope of this paper to determine the future presence of the Syrian refugees in the host countries, we conduct analysis and make policy suggestions, bearing in mind how steps could meet short-term needs and long-term needs, while upholding the hopes of both the Syrians and their host countries that many of the Syrians will be able to return home.

Study Approach, Limitations, and Organization of the Report

This report provides an overview of the circumstances and policy considerations of education of Syrian refugees in Lebanon, Turkey, and Jordan. The research approach included a literature review of refugee education around the world and a document review of refugee education in the countries studied, including public documents and studies provided by governments, UN agencies, and nongovernmental organizations (NGOs) in Turkey, Lebanon, and Jordan. While the Syrian situation—and all refugee situations—are unique, many of the particular challenges faced in the Syrian education crisis have also been faced in other refugee crises. The study also drew on more than 35 interviews with government agencies (ministries of education and planning), UN agencies (including UNHCR, UNICEF, and others), donors, NGOs and think tanks, and school principals, conducted in the three countries between July and August 2014.

This report has limitations. First, it is a scoping study, intended to provide an overview of trends across the three countries, rather than an in-depth analysis of each country. Next, ten to 15 stakeholder interviews were conducted in each country with key stakeholders that included government officials, donors, UN agencies, and NGOs; not all stakeholders were available for interviews in each country. Finally, available data sources about refugee education are incomplete in some cases. To address these limitations, the report acknowledges where information is not fully available and combines information from several sources.

To organize the analysis and consider practical steps involved in addressing Syrian refugee education, we developed an applied, functional framework for managing refugee education, depicted in Figure 1.3.

The framework includes policy considerations in four areas of refugee education:

- **Access:** How can refugee children access education?
- **Management:** How will refugee education be planned, managed, and resourced?
- **Society:** How can refugee education promote a stable and prosperous society? How can plans for refugee education be managed within sensitive political constraints?
- **Quality:** How can the quality of education for both refugees and host-country citizens be promoted in such difficult circumstances?

The refugee education framework developed for this report stems from (1) the issues listed as most important by interviewees, (2) our review of conclusions of the literature, and (3) elements included in

Figure 1.3
A Functional Framework for Syrian Refugee Education

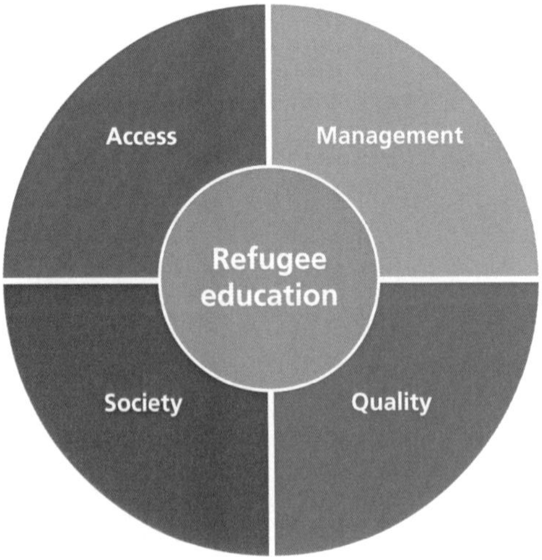

RAND RR859-1.3

other education frameworks. UNHCR's *Refugee Education: A Global Review*, structures discussion around access, quality, and protection (Dryden-Peterson, 2011). The International Network for Education in Emergencies (INEE) adopted a set of minimum standards in emergency education, organized into five domains: foundational standards (similar to our quality element); access and learning environment (similar to our access element); teaching and learning (overlaps with our quality and society element); teachers and other educational personnel (overlaps with our management element); and education policy (overlaps with our quality and management elements) (INEE, 2010). The Refugee Studies Center at Oxford University uses a framework of supply and demand (similar to our access element), gaps, and good practices (overlaps with our management and quality elements) (Chatty, 2015). Quality and access are thus common elements of education frameworks. The element of "society" in our framework is based on analysis of the social, demographic, and political issues we found during the study. The element of "management" comes from the many discussions about the multiple coordination challenges and complexities in refugee education.

In line with the functional framework, this report is organized into six chapters. After this introduction, Chapter Two argues that there is a crisis of access to education, and that improving access to out-of-school Syrian children should be the primary focus of host governments, UN agencies, and donors. Chapter Three provides context about management of refugee education, describes information gaps and needs, and makes the case for long-term development planning in addition to shorter-term humanitarian responses. Chapter Four discusses education and society. It proposes deliberative decisionmaking about how to integrate education for social cohesion, suggests developing evidence-based employment policies that take into account host country unemployment and economic considerations and the need of Syrians for livelihoods, and describes the need for an approach to certification. Chapter Five describes challenges to quality education, for host-country education systems and for the refugees, and proposes steps to mitigate challenges. Finally, in Chapter Six, we conclude by calling for a coordinated, cost-effective strategy to address Syrian refugee education, to delineate the many conflicting goals and assumptions for how these education needs should be met, and to note the unfortunate but unavoidable need for trade-offs.

CHAPTER TWO

Access

The low rate of access to education for Syrian refugees is a crisis. While Lebanon, Turkey, and Jordan all set policies that enable Syrian refugees to have access to public education, enrollment is low and actual attendance is unknown. Many children have been out of school for several years because after their education was interrupted in Syria, a lack of stable access in the host countries followed. Lack of education threatens to create a generation of Syrian children without the life and job skills they need for the future. In this chapter, we describe education access policies, data, and rates for formal education; barriers to access and efforts to address the barriers; alternative education programs; and policy considerations for access, recommending a focused regional approach to improve access through infrastructure investment, sustained financing, and problem-solving.

Access Policies, Data, and Rates for Formal Education

Access to formal education is low, varies according to location and setting (camps or host communities), and is difficult to quantify with accuracy. Figure 2.1 shows estimates for Syrian refugee enrollment in formal education in March 2015 (3RP, 2015b).

Enrollment of Syrian refugees in formal education at the beginning of the 2014 school year was about 25 percent in Lebanon (with 102,000 Syrian children enrolled, out of an estimated 408,000 school-age children), about 60 percent in Turkey (200,500 Syrian children enrolled out of an estimated 345,500 school-age children), and 60 per-

Figure 2.1
School Enrollment of Syrian Refugees in Lebanon, Turkey, and Jordan in 2015

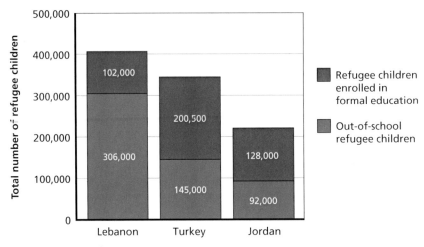

SOURCE: 3RP, 2015b.
RAND RR859-2.1

cent in Jordan (128,000 enrolled out of an estimated 220,000 school age children). In sum, about 44 percent of registered Syrian school-age children were enrolled in formal education in these three countries as of March 2015.[1] This percentage is lower than the international average of refugee enrollment in primary school (76 percent) and secondary school (36 percent) (Dryden-Peterson, 2011). A crucial consideration has been the speed at which the Syrian refugee numbers have grown, along with the large numbers of refugees, difficult for host countries to absorb.

The enrollment rates in formal education were higher in camps than in host communities in 2014 in Turkey; the opposite was the case in Jordan. In Turkey in 2014, enrollment rates of Syrian refugee school-age children were 80 percent in camps and 27 percent in host communities, according to one needs assessment (Dorman, 2014).

---

[1] Note that numbers of school-age Syrian refugee children used later in this report are updated and larger; the enrollment proportions used here from August 2014 across countries were the latest available that were comparable in nature.

Delving down into specific host communities in Turkey, International Medical Corps (IMC) surveys conducted in 2014 found that only 17 percent of school-age refugee children were enrolled in school in Istanbul (IMC, 2014b) and 16 percent in Gaziantep (IMC, 2014a). A survey by AFAD Turkey's governmental body responsible for refugees, found that only 14 percent of refugees in host communities were actually attending school in 2013 (AFAD, 2013). In Jordan in 2014, enrollment in formal education was 52 percent in the Zaatari Camp and 62 percent in host communities (Renewed Efforts Against Child Hunger [REACH], 2014a; REACH, 2015). Lebanon does not have formal camps; its urban enrollment rate, as already stated, was 25 percent in 2015. Enrollment and attendance data are not consistent at times, for a number of reasons.

While these figures demonstrate that access is low, a particular challenge is precisely quantifying access rates and reasons for lack of access, data that are important for planning and problem-solving. These measurements are difficult to attain for several reasons. First, the refugee influx has been ongoing, with steadily increasing numbers entering each country starting in 2011 and continuing as of this writing. Thus, statistics on the continuing stream of refugees change frequently. Second, not all of the refugees have registered with the appropriate authorities or with international humanitarian organizations, so the total number of refugees in each country is not known with certainty. For example, UNHCR estimates the number of refugees in Jordan at 630,000, while Jordan's Ministry of Interior (MOI) announced a planning figure of 1.4 million ("Prince El-Hassan: Syrian Refugees Crisis Requires National-Level Thinking," 2014). Similarly, interviewees in Turkey and Lebanon also indicated that the numbers of registered refugees are below the actual numbers. Third, governments, UN agencies, and NGOs have been actively seeking to enroll refugee children, and their success in this endeavor means that enrollment rates continuously increase. Fourth, while there are data on enrollment in each country, interviewees noted that there is little aggregated information on actual attendance. Finally, while there are education surveys in Zaatari and host communities in Jordan, comprehensive education surveys of the refugees in Turkey and Lebanon are lacking. Even with these challenges, the data strongly point to an access problem.

Barriers to Formal Education

Refugees face multiple barriers to educational access. Interviewees for this study, as well as UNICEF's report *Shattered Lives* (UNICEF, 2013a) identified such concerns as school space shortages, language barriers, lack of transportation, registration requirements, prioritization of survival, belief in imminent return to Syria, expenses, bullying, and tensions at school. There has not been a comprehensive survey to date to quantify the extent or relative importance of each barrier in Turkey and Lebanon, although surveys have been conducted in Jordan (REACH, 2014a; REACH, 2015; UNHCR, 2014b). We discuss these challenges and some of the solutions that have been brought to bear.

School space shortages may be the biggest obstacle. While Syrians have increased Jordan's population by 10–20 percent, they are disproportionately concentrated in regions near the Syrian borders and in poor urban areas elsewhere in Jordan. This places strains on schools in those regions and neighborhoods. By the 2013–2014 school year, 98 Jordanian schools added a second shift to accommodate refugee children, according to Jordan's Ministry of Education (MOE). In 2014, the MOE announced a need to build 72 additional schools to support the refugees ("Jordan Needs 72 New Schools to Accommodate Refugee Children—Majali," 2014). In Lebanon, there is now more demand for public school spaces for Syrian children than for Lebanese children (UNHCR, 2014e). Because 70 percent of Lebanese children attend private schools, this means around 275,000 Lebanese children attend public schools, compared with 408,000 required spaces for Syrian children (UNICEF, 2013b). To accommodate the additional students, Lebanon is adding second shifts to schools for Syrian students. Government interviewees there also mentioned plans to add another 100,000 school spaces for Syrians, provided that donor funding is available. (Other interviewees put forward the observation that Syrians had set up schools of their own because of the lack of formal school spaces, but information on this is limited.) Both Lebanon and Jordan have conducted outreach campaigns to increase access; however, interviewees noted that the outreach campaigns at times result in demand for more school spaces than are available, leading to wait lists. Meeting the demand depends on using available school spaces and creating new ones. Complexities involved in both of these approaches (including infrastructure, teachers and staff, budget, and relations with host communities) is discussed in the policy implications.

Language and curriculum are barriers to school enrollment in Turkey and Lebanon, and to a smaller extent in Jordan (INEE, 2014). In Turkey, Turkish is the language of instruction and few Syrian children (previously educated in Arabic) enroll in the Turkish public school system. UNHCR interviewees said that only 8,500 Syrian students (out of the 345,500 Syrian school-age children) were enrolled in Turkish public schools in the 2013–2014 school year. Because of the language barriers, UNICEF built 40 schools in areas with large numbers of Syrians; these schools operate in Arabic and in double shifts to accommodate the demand for spaces (Dorman, 2014; Mekki, 2013). In addition, Syrian refugees have set up ad hoc, unregulated community schools in other available buildings. There are no data about the numbers of community schools or children in them, although interviewees estimated that there were at least 60 such schools for the 2014–2015 school year and noted that Turkey's Ministry of National Education (MONE) had plans to survey them. In this case, differences in language and curriculum contribute to school space shortages in Turkey, as refugee education policies and Syrian preferences are for enrollment in Arab-language schools, of which there are few in proportion to the numbers of Syrians.

The Lebanese curriculum is in three languages—Arabic, French, and English, similarly posing difficulties for Syrian children. To address this, Lebanese public schools teach the English and French parts of the curriculum in Arabic for the Syrians. Interviewees described challenges for Lebanese teachers not used to teaching these subjects in Arabic. In Jordan, language is less of a barrier: The Jordanian curriculum is in Arabic, although it expects greater levels of English proficiency than does the Syrian curriculum.

Integration to secondary-school curricula has been particularly challenging for older students. As in other refugee situations elsewhere in the world—international averages are 76 percent enrollment for primary school and 36 percent enrollment in secondary, as described above (Dryden-Peterson, 2011)—all three countries have even lower rates of enrollment at the secondary level than at the primary level. Interviewees stated that older children find it more difficult to cope with a new curriculum. For example, in Lebanon, only 1,000 Syrians were enrolled in secondary school in 2014, according to Lebanon's Ministry of Education and Higher Education (MEHE). Enrollment of Syrian children is higher for kindergarten through third grade, then drops incrementally in each grade following.

Indeed, language and curriculum for refugee education is a debated issue in other refugee crises as well. Some argue for education of the refugees in the language and curriculum of their home country (Sinclair, 2001; INEE, 2010). Others argue for integration into the education system of the host country for cases in which refugees reside in host communities, even if that means education in a new language and curriculum. Still others promote basing this decision upon context (Dryden-Peterson, 2011). This issue will be further discussed in Chapter Four.

Transportation is expensive, often not available outside of camps, and perceived as not safe by refugee parents for their children (especially girls) in all three countries (INEE, 2014). In Jordan, there is no public school transportation system, and interviewees stated that some students who are offered school spaces do not attend because of the lack of school buses or the expense of public buses or taxis. Lack of school transportation is also a challenge faced by Jordanians. In Lebanon, interviewees estimate that in many cases, the cost of transportation is as much as the cost per child of attending school, thus limiting what the government or donors can provide. Similarly, in Turkey, students have difficulties securing transportation to the Syrian community schools and UNICEF schools. The consequences have been troubling—especially for girls; sometimes family members do not permit girls to attend school because of the lengthy travel distance required (UNICEF, 2013a).

Registration status and parental documentation is an additional barrier. In Jordan and Turkey, parental documentation is required for children to register in public schools. NGO interviewees said that there are cases of some families not being able to enroll children in school in Jordan because of lack of a required registration with the MOI. In Turkey, access to public schools has required a passport, registration with the police, and a residence permit, conditions met by a small minority of refugees (Dinçer et al., 2013). In December 2014, Turkey issued new policies for the Syrian refugees, with an enhanced set of rights that reduced the obstacle of registration for education, allowing Syrians with several different types of registration status to enroll (Yeginsu, 2014).

Child labor and early marriage are indicators that survival is taking precedence over education. In some cases, access to food and shelter are so fragile that education is either not possible or not prioritized. A survey of refugees in Istanbul found that education is a secondary priority in comparison with food, shelter, and health (IMC, 2014b). For both boys and girls, but especially boys, working has substituted for schooling to help the family meet basic needs. One in ten refugee children are estimated to be working instead of attending school (UNHCR, 2014a). Children have various occupations, including selling goods, begging, waiting in lines to receive aid, and working in construction or cleaning. In Jordan, MOE interviewees note that the number of boys enrolled in school is half of the number of girls. Similarly, in a survey of the Akkar region in Lebanon, the enrollment of Syrian boys in school was half that of girls (REACH, 2014b). Low rates for boys also could be because some are fighting in Syria. A recent study found that in 47 percent of households that reported paid employment, a child contributed to the household income. Early marriage for girls is also on the rise because of economic hardship. UNICEF announced that while child marriage accounted for 13 percent of marriages in Syria before 2011, it accounts for 32 percent of Syrian marriages in Jordan now ("Child Marriages Double Among Syrian Refugees in Jordan," 2014).

Expenses, or perception of expenses, were cited by interviewees as possibly prohibiting school attendance—including school fees, uniforms, transportation, or food. While UN agencies or NGOs provide support for these fees in some cases, many refugees either do not know about this support or lack access to it. For example, one refugee interviewed for this study in Lebanon said that his five children did not attend school in part because of fees; he did not know that UNHCR provided payment for the fees.

School environments also may pose obstacles. In surveys, parents note tensions in school between Syrian students and students and staff of the host country. There are reports of bullying both among Syrians and between Syrians and host-country children. Syrian children have been through traumatic events and may come from parts of Syria with strained relations. Refugees tend to be especially vulnerable because of their status and they are likely to be perceived as a burden by some of the citizens (UNICEF, 2013a).

Grade placement is difficult in these circumstances. The classroom environment can include children at multiple school levels; some children who have been out of school for several years are embarrassed to find themselves in classrooms with younger children. Jordan's MOE prohibits children who have been out of school for three years or more from enrolling in formal classrooms. Programs for children who have missed several years of school have yet to be designed at the scale needed in any country.

Alternative Educational Programs

In addition to formal education, there are various alternative educational programs in all three countries. These are a mix of programs run by NGOs, private individuals, the Syrian community, and religious organizations. These alternative educational programs range in content, including programs for recreational arts and sports, tutoring programs to help children who have missed periods of school adapt to new curricula or catch up to their grade level, religious education in mosques, skills and language training programs, and programs meant to substitute for the formal classroom setting.

Programs, definitions, and use of terms vary across countries. For example, in Jordan, the MOE has defined three main categories of education for the refugees: formal (in public school classes), nonformal (the MOE curriculum delivered at home or in centers for older students who have been out of school for three or more years), and informal (remedial support during formal education and catch-up education to help students re-enter school after a prolonged absence) ("Glossary of Education Services," 2014). There are also discussions under way among the international assistance community in Jordan about the need for additional alternative programs to address more than 90,000 children who are not accommodated in the formal education system because of space constraints; it is not yet clear what the curriculum, funding source, or design of these programs would be. Programs in Lebanon include alternative learning programs (education programs not related to acquiring certification from formal education), catch-up programs (programs covering missed material to help children who have been out of school re-enter formal education), remedial (tutoring to help refugee children stay in formal education), and community-based education (for children out of school, with Syrian teachers). In all three countries, interviewees noted that in some cases, mosques have been providing education for out-of-school children; little information is available about the quality, content, political messaging, or reach of these programs.

Interviewees in all three countries noted little evidence regarding the effectiveness of alternative educational programs; to date, there have been few assessments of quality. Also unclear and unarticulated about these programs as a group is how they fit into an education-employment pathway, and how participation in such programs provides children the means to acquire needed skills for life as an adult, to enter a formal certified education pathway at a later point, or to have skills needed later for employment. NGOs have been creating their own curricula separately; it is not clear that this duplication is a sound use of resources and how these curricula meet national quality standards and goals. Some interviewees also raised concerns about the political content that may be prevalent in some of these programs, although little is known about political messaging in alternative education.

Policy Considerations

Develop a coordinated strategy to address access for out-of-school children. We argue that the most urgent need is for a coordinated strategy for access to formal education (whether provided by a government or another entity) for out-of-school Syrian children, particularly at the primary level. Educational quality and protection cannot be provided without first having access to education. At least 542,000 school-age Syrian refugee children in Lebanon, Turkey, and Jordan are not enrolled in formal school. Low rates of school enrollment among the Syrian refugees is the greatest cause for concern about their future, as well as the futures of Syrian society and host-country societies. A generation of children is growing up without stable access to quality education—a lost generation. Education for refugees is defined as a right in United Nations resolutions, and is vital to individual children.[2] Education enables students to gain the knowledge and skills they will need as productive adults, and it provides students with needed protection and community.

Providing this education will be no easy endeavor. The needed strategy will be complex and resource intensive, and will require coordinated management and diplomacy. It calls for speed, as a generation of children is losing time out of school, as well as medium-term thinking, as many of these children will be in their host countries for the foreseeable future. An access expansion strategy must accommodate multiple complexities of the refugee situation, including the quick growth in numbers, cost-effectiveness, and flexibility to adapt to the unknown future of the refugees' status either in returning to Syria or remaining in the host countries. It requires developing new approaches to formal education for children who have missed up to several years

---

[2]   See the UN Convention on human rights for universal right to primary education (1948) and the Convention on the rights of the child, right to education for refugees (1989), as well as Article 22 of the Convention relating to the Status of Refugees (1951), Resolution 64/290 of the Human Rights Council of the United Nations General Assembly on the right to education in emergencies (United Nations, 2010b), and the draft resolution to the Human Rights Council on the right to education for refugees, migrants, and asylum seekers (United Nations, 2010b).

of school. It depends on balancing the delicate political considerations described in Chapter One. It also requires consideration of trade-offs among access, quality, political feasibility, and government capacity.

We present options for elements of an access strategy (Figure 2.2). These include strategic use of more available school spaces; strengthening government management capacity; addressing barriers to access and creating high-quality, consistent formal alternatives to government-provided education; and development of building plans. We also suggest further analysis and study of these options for cost-effectiveness per child; how well options meet short-term objectives of increasing access for children; ways of preserving countries' rights to base planning on the assumption that the Syrians will go home; and how they meet needs of a longer-term scenario in which Syrians stay for several decades. All of these require a medium- to long-term financing plan, discussed in more depth in Chapter Three. A final note is that an access plan is intimately tied up with management, social cohesion, and quality. Subsequent chapters will discuss the complexities of these aspects in greater depth.

Figure 2.2
Options for a Strategy for Education Access for Out-of-School Syrians

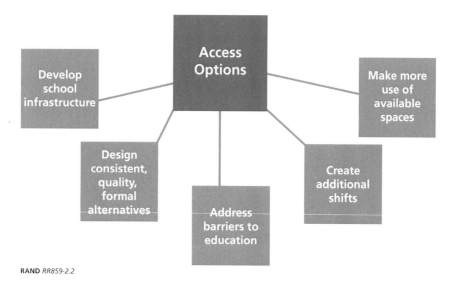

Develop a plan to make strategic use of more available school spaces. Because of the rapid growth in the numbers of refugees, what has not occurred is a mapping (for example, using geographic information system [GIS] mapping) of where the school-age refugees are in relation to available school spaces in the host countries. This is particularly important for the host communities, as refugees are dispersed. Based on this comparative mapping of where the refugees and additional spaces are, transportation systems could be developed to distribute refugees among available school spaces when spaces are not available near where they live. This could include development by the donor community of a busing program to distribute the refugee children among schools until there has been time to build new buildings or repurpose other buildings as needed. While there are examples of occasional, small transportation programs, a scaled-up approach to transportation is needed. For example, interviewees in Jordan noted high concentrations of Syrians in some schools, while other schools in the same communities had very few. A survey of the border region of Akkar in Lebanon found school spaces could be made available if there were coordination to match children with space availability (REACH, 2014b). Community relations are a consideration in this recommendation; citizens likely will feel resentment if Syrians are offered school transportation while their own children are not. A donor-funded or developed transportation plan would need to consider this issue in its design; a transportation plan that included host-country children in neighborhoods served would also leave the host communities with a benefit.

This option has the most potential in Jordan. Jordan shares a common language with the Syrians; many Syrians have been integrated into Jordanian public schools; and the Syrians as a whole make up 10–20 percent of the population in Jordan. In Turkey, Syrians are mostly attending schools set up for Syrians, not public schools, as discussed further in Chapter Four. In Lebanon, where there are more school-age Syrians than Lebanese children in public schools, fewer spaces are available.

Create additional shifts in public schools, with greater attention to quality. Continue to create additional double-shifts in public schools. In terms of infrastructure, this could be done in all three countries, making use of existing school buildings. It has the advantage that infrastructure already exists and could be scaled up rapidly. Challenges and risks include how (and whether) to integrate Syrian children and host-country children, hiring teachers, adequate instructional time, host-country citizen dissatisfaction with shifts, and curriculum choice (mainly in Turkey). In Jordan and Lebanon, hiring enough teachers for new shifts has not been a constraint, as governments have hired unemployed college graduates; Syrians who were teachers could also be hired. In Turkey, many Syrian refugees who were teachers could also be hired. However, opening additional shifts in government schools creates additional costs for governments. Direct bilateral financing for such an expansion would be needed—for example, to cover teacher salaries, building maintenance, and utilities. The following chapters further discuss these challenges and ways to mitigate the management, social cohesion, and quality risks of double-shift schools.

Develop consistent, quality, full-time, certified formal educational alternatives. To varying extents, all three countries face capacity challenges in providing formal education to the Syrians in government schools. When the public school systems cannot accommodate the children, the international community should assess options to complement government efforts with structured, certified, full-time alternative education programs for the Syrians. These alternative programs should not be the current mix of programs, which are disconnected in goals, quality monitoring, what is taught, and provision. Rather, they should be coordinated to fund efforts that would serve as an equivalent to certified formal education. This could mean finding ways to fund Syrian-run schools sustainably, private schools opened by the private sector, schools operated by NGOs, or other innovative approaches. This entails establishing quality standards, monitoring quality, and ensuring adequate instructional time; e.g., the Organisation for Economic Co-Operation and Development [OECD] average is 800 hours of instructional time per year (OECD, 2009). Such programs should support and complement formal education in a recognized curriculum—the Syrian curriculum, a host-country curriculum, or other curriculum. This is happening to some extent in Turkey, although without quality monitoring. In Lebanon, there is a long history of private schools operating a significant part (70 percent) of the education system. Such alternative programs could make further use of the Syrian refugees who were teachers. In Jordan, alternative education is provided and becoming more standardized, although it lacks clear pathways and links to formal education.

Analyze scope of barriers to access, and develop plans to address them. While studies have collected qualitative descriptions of barriers, few studies have collected data on the extent or importance of each of the barriers, particularly in Turkey and Lebanon. These data are needed to inform a plan to solve problems. We surmise that this may primarily mean six areas of action (some of which are under way) based on the interviews and literature review: increasing school spaces, offering transportation to available school spaces, conducting outreach campaigns in coordination with school space availability, changing policies to allow Syrian children to register in schools regardless of parent registration status, offering extended catch-up support for out-of-school children, establishing formal programs for children who have been out of school for several years, and enabling parents to work to reduce the need for children to work and for girls to marry early.

Pursue an innovative school financing and building plan. Lack of school infrastructure is an obstacle to scaling up education programs and providing more school spaces. A school building strategy should include (1) facilitation to the extent possible of both short- and longer-term scenarios, (2) repurposing of buildings, (3) building additional schools, (4) innovative medium- or long-term financing, and (5) global and regional longer-term commitments.

As discussed in Chapter One, many Syrian refugees will likely remain in their host countries for the foreseeable future, even up to several decades. At the same time, it is infeasible for governments to publicly acknowledge this. An infrastructure plan that could meet both short-term and longer-term requirements is needed so that governments can describe their plans as short-term while giving options to meet their educational needs sustainably in the future. Using a combination of existing infrastructure and new infrastructure would enable education to be ramped up or down quickly. While double-shifted schools can serve as part of the solution, more school buildings will be required to accommodate additional children.

In addition to double shifts at existing schools, buildings not originally built as schools could be used on a temporary basis; this could be accomplished by assessing building spaces in areas with high concentrations of refugees and renting and repurposing those buildings found to be acceptable. While this is not ideal in the long term (for example, with architecture not designed to support educational goals or lacking recess space), access needs are so great that they outweigh these considerations. Using buildings on a temporary basis also would allow school programs to be reduced if the Syrians go home.

Building plans could also leave the countries with a benefit of additional infrastructure. Even without the addition of the Syrians, Lebanon and Jordan were in need of higher-quality and additional school buildings; investment in buildings could serve that purpose. Faster and less-expensive construction methods, such as prefabricated buildings, also can help mitigate this need.

Innovative longer-term financing methods could include, for example, public-private partnerships (PPPs), in which private companies finance and construct buildings in exchange for the government leasing the building over time. This is a viable approach for governments facing capital shortages, and invites private-sector investment. This financing method has been used for schools and public infrastructure around the world, including in Egypt and the United Kingdom (Pryor, 2006; "Schools Pilot Launched," 2006; Stainback and Donahue, 2005). It has been particularly effective in the face of public capital funding shortages and when a robust private sector has the capability for building and financing.

Furthermore, as the scope and scale of the crisis continues to increase, it is important to recognize the global and regional responsibilities in financing the response, including in education. Donor commitments for refugee education (from traditional donors, such as the United States and the European Union, as well as regional Gulf donors) should move from short-term programmatic funding to longer-term commitments, including financing infrastructure, to support the host governments.

CHAPTER THREE

Management

Management of Syrian refugee education is complex, challenging to coordinate among stakeholders, time sensitive, and resource intensive. In this chapter, we provide an overview of management of Syrian refugee education, how it is resourced, and data to support management and decisionmaking. We make the case for long-term development planning in addition to short-term humanitarian responses. This chapter also recommends additional information strategies to support effective management of refugee education.

Roles and Responsibilities

Syrian refugee education involves actors working in multiple roles in education provision; school facilities and supplies; teacher supply and training; monitoring, oversight, and information; overarching policy-setting and resourcing; and supportive functions. Responsibility for these roles rests primarily with national governments, UN agencies, donors, NGOs, and the refugees themselves. Table 3.1 diagrams these roles.

Some of the functions described are traditional responsibilities of governments in education in normal times but have been taken on by UN agencies and NGOs during this crisis; for example, provision of education, starting new schools, and data collection. Many of these responsibilities are specific to the short-term needs of the humanitarian crisis and may only be needed for several years until capacity has expanded to be able to absorb the Syrian children into formal education, or until some of the Syrians go home.

Table 3.1
Entities and their Roles and Responsibilities in Syrian Refugee Education

Roles and Responsibilities	Governments	UN Agencies	NGOs	Donors	Refugees
Education provision					
Formal education in host communities	X	X		X	
Formal education in camps and UN schools	X	X		X	
Alternative education provision		X	X	X	X
School facilities and supplies					
Provision of school supplies and school fees		X	X		X
Improving existing school facilities to accommodate additional students	X	X	X	X	
Starting new schools (construction, hiring of teachers, materials)	X	X		X	
Teacher supply and training					
Psychosocial training of teachers	X	X	X		
Volunteering or working as teachers in formal or informal education					X
Monitoring, oversight, and information					
Formal education	X				
NGOs	X	X		X	
Data collection	X	X	X		
Overarching policy-setting and resourcing					
Funding	X	X		X	X
Decisions about curriculum modifications and graduation certificates for refugees	X	X			
Policy coordination of national and international actors	X	X		X	
Supportive functions		X	X		X

Roles in Education Provision

National governments in Jordan and Lebanon provide school spaces in formal public schools to refugees in host communities, integrating refugees into public schools and establishing second shifts for the refugees. In Jordan, UN agencies and the MOE are jointly managing schools within the refugee camps in Jordan, using the Jordanian MOE curriculum. In Lebanon, interviewees noted that the Syrian community had started schools, and that the private school sector may be filling some of the formal education gaps, although information is lacking about the extent of these approaches. In Turkey, the MONE has taken a smaller role in provision of formal education for the refugees; UNICEF established and manages 40 schools for refugees in host communities, as well as additional schools in the camps, and the Syrian refugee community has established an unknown number (estimated by interviewees as perhaps 60 by 2014) of community schools as well. As mentioned previously, alternative education provision is emerging in all three countries as a means to accommodate the large number of refugees who cannot attend school in the already overwhelmed government formal school systems. These alternative options are provided by UN agencies, NGOs, religious organizations, and the refugees themselves.

Roles in School Facilities and Supplies

The needs for school facilities and supplies have been filled by a collection of organizations and entities operating in the refugee education arena. Host governments in Jordan and Lebanon have expanded existing facilities or offered double shifts to accommodate new students, refurbished some schools, and built new ones. In Turkey, provinces and private individuals have provided school space for the Syrian schools. The UN agencies have funded and overseen existing facility renovation, new construction, and providing school supplies. In Turkey, UNICEF oversaw construction of 40 prefabricated schools. In Jordan, UNICEF provided 69 schools with furniture and equipment, and 65 schools with prefabricated additions. Donor countries and organizations have also played an important role in funding existing or new school facilities. Due to limited access to resources, NGOs and refugees have been more involved in providing supplies and rehabilitating existing facilities rather than new construction.

Roles in Teacher Supply and Training

Most of the teacher supply in Jordan and Lebanon in formal education has been from the government, and have been Jordanian and Lebanese teachers. In Jordan, Syrians are not allowed to be hired as teachers but are allowed to work as teaching assistants in the camp schools, although not in host-community schools. Their role is viewed as serving as intermediaries between the Syrian children and the newly hired Jordanian teachers, who typically are inexperienced recent university graduates and are less familiar with the recent difficult experiences of Syrian children. In Lebanon, there is no official role for Syrians as teachers, although there are an unknown number of Syrian community schools, about which little is known. In Turkey, Syrian refugees worked as unpaid teachers in 2014 (although some had volunteer stipends) in the Syrian community and UNICEF schools. Funding to expand hiring of teachers and teacher salaries is lacking in all three countries.

The need for teacher training is significant. Host country governments, UN agencies, and NGOs all have been engaging in training on curricular and pedagogical topics and addressing the psychosocial needs of the children.

Roles in Monitoring, Oversight, and Information

Another role has been in monitoring—both the formal education that the refugee children are receiving as well as the alternative programs. The formal education being provided falls largely under the supervision of the host-country governments. In Jordan and Lebanon, governments monitor the public schools and the second shifts; interviewees reported lower levels of quality monitoring for the second shifts. In Turkey, interviewees noted in 2014 that MONE had yet to establish a set of quality standards and oversight system for the Syrian community schools, while UNICEF and MONE jointly monitored the UNICEF schools. UN agencies and donors, as well as host-country governments to some extent, monitor NGOs in the alternative provision, since in many cases they are funding NGO programs and activities. However, systematic educational standards and monitoring are lacking for alternative education across all three countries. Data collection is done by governments, UN agencies, and NGOs, and is discussed in further detail later in this chapter.

There was concern among interviewees that a substantial portion of education provision is occurring without appropriate oversight, as government capacity for comprehensive oversight and monitoring is limited and policies and systems have not been established for schools, shifts, and alternative programs for the refugees.

Roles in Overarching Policy-Setting and Resourcing

Governments, UN agencies, and donors have responsibility for over-arching policy-setting, coordinating, resourcing, and advocacy. UNHCR also has taken the lead on coordinating multiple actors in writing regional and national refugee response plans. UNICEF is responsible for coordinating much of the education response, funding NGO work, and funding refugee schools in the camps. UN agencies also have held responsibility in interagency coordination structures for education in the three countries. While refugee education was primarily coordinated by UN agencies in the beginning of the crisis, the government of Lebanon, in particular MEHE, stepped forward to take primary responsibility for coordinating education in Lebanon with donors, UN agencies, and NGOs. In Jordan, UNICEF and Save the Children lead coordination of the Education Sector Working Group.

In terms of curriculum and degree requirements, the governments of Jordan and Lebanon have expanded use of their countries' national curricula for the refugees, and the government of Turkey worked with UN agencies and the Syrian opposition to develop and put in place the "Syrian Adapted Curriculum" for the refugees, discussed further in Chapter Four. UN agencies and NGOs also have been involved in developing and implementing curricula for alternative education, and both host-country governments and UN agencies have worked together to identify solutions for granting secondary-school graduation certificates. Some interviewees expressed concern about the quality of the curriculum in alternative programming across countries and the political affiliations of the Syrian Adapted Curriculum in Turkey. There was also concern about potential for groups running some schools to foster religious and political environments that may be incompatible with the host country's policies.

Governments have funded expansion of their education systems to accommodate the refugees. Donor countries and UN agencies provide additional funding for supportive measures. Some of the largest donors for refugee education among the three countries are the United States, Kuwait, the European Union, Germany, the Republic of Korea, Japan, Canada, and the United Arab Emirates, according to interviewees. The United States Agency for International Development is the largest education donor in Jordan, with ongoing development programs in addition to aid specifically for the crisis. UN agencies have overseen use of funds, in many cases to NGOs, to implement programs and provide services. Among the refugees, some individuals with resources have contributed funds for education, and refugees bear some of the fees for books, school supplies, and transportation associated with attending school. Government, UN, and donor interviewees across countries noted problems with transparency of funding, and little consistent accounting of how much funding is coming from which sources and going to which entities.

To date, much of the resources and management invested in the refugee education response has been for shorter-term, more-urgent needs of the refugees, with gaps in investment in governments' capabilities to provide formal education, as discussed later, or other entities' capabilities to provide formal alternative education.

Roles in Supportive Functions

There have been a number of additional supportive activities, including outreach and registration support for children to enter formal education, management of child-friendly spaces, referrals to other services (such as health, housing, food, etc.), advocacy with families against child labor and early marriage, social workers and psychologists in schools and registration points, collection of data, help-desks and referral points in the communities, and problem-solving support.[1] NGOs

---

[1]   Leading NGOs in Jordan, as described in the Regional Response Plan 6 (RRP6), include: Agency for Technical Cooperation and Development (ACTED), Caritas, Danish Refugee

typically implement and are funded and managed largely by UN agencies, although some NGOs have outside funding. In some cases, there is overlap in NGO and UN agency activity. For example, UNICEF may be funding NGO implementation of child-friendly spaces, but UNICEF is also a provider. NGOs include international and national organizations, religious-based organizations, and government-sponsored agencies. Syrian refugees have been involved in outreach and registration to boost enrollment in formal education settings.

Plans and Budgets

To address education needs, entities have coordinated to develop plans at both the national and regional levels. Plans have evolved over time in their strategic approach. They reflected short-term humanitarian programs in the first years of the crisis. The 2015 3RP shifted this approach to recognize need for investment in the medium-term development of capabilities of host governments and communities to manage refugee education themselves over time, which the 3RP calls "resilience." (Yet while planning documents reflected these changes in goals, interviewees in 2015 expressed confusion about what "resilience" means in practical terms when bridging short-term humanitarian responses with longer-term responses that integrate host communities.)

Regional response plans have been coordinated by UNHCR and include objectives, targets, budgets, and calls for international funding to manage education and other sectors of the refugee response (UNHCR, 2014e). The budget requested for the 2014 RRP6 was $3.74 billion; 53 percent of the budget request was received in each sector (3RP, 2015c; UNHCR, 2014e). The education request was $397 million, 11 percent of the total budget. Most of the requested refugee edu-

---

Council, Madrasati Initiative, Mercy Corps, Norwegian Refugee Council, Questscope, Relief International, Save the Children, and others. Leading NGOs in Lebanon described in the RRP6 include: Norwegian Refugee Council, Relief International, Save the Children, and others. The RRP6 does not describe particular NGOs in leading roles in Turkey, although a number are providing support, such as Save the Children, Mercycorps, Catholic Relief Services, International Medical Corps, and others. See UNHCR (2014e).

cation budget in the RRP6 was allocated for UN agencies and NGOs for the urgent short-term humanitarian education response, and not for direct budget support to the governments, as shown in Figure 3.1 (UNHCR, 2014e). The RRP6 included a small amount of requested support for the government of Lebanon, but none for Jordan or Turkey.

Governments also made separate plans and bilateral funding requests to the international community. Both Jordan and Lebanon published national policies and strategies for refugee education. Overviews of Jordan's response across sectors, including education, is the 2014 National Resilience Plan (MOPIC, 2014a) and the 2015 Jordan Response Plan (MOPIC, 2015). Lebanon released a plan entitled *Reaching All Children with Education in Lebanon* that lays out an education strategy (MEHE, 2014b). Such a public document for refugee education was not available in Turkey, although interviewees noted that Turkey's MONE is starting a planning process to develop a framework for Syrian refugee education.

While the bilateral requests were important, the 2014 RRP6 did not give the added weight of including national government budgeting

Figure 3.1
Education Budget Requests for the 2014 Regional Response Plan 6

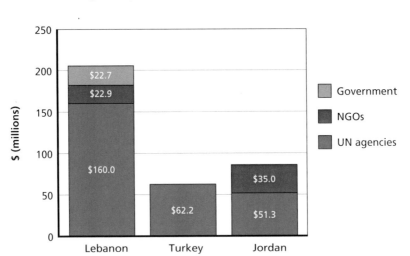

SOURCE: UNHCR, 2014d.

RAND RR859-3.1

in the coordinated UN-backed budget requests to the international community, except for a proportionally small amount for Lebanon. While the multilateral and NGO responses provided vital humanitarian support, that support may not have translated into countries' capabilities to provide the elements of formal education, such as school buildings, teachers, supplies, training, and more, in the medium to long term. These issues attracted significant donor support in the beginning. Yet, as the crisis drags on, there is a risk of donor fatigue and the funds dwindling.

This approach of treating the refugee crisis as something that could be handled without longer-term considerations for the host community gained recognition as being unsustainable. Interviewees and reports alike described growing recognition of the likely long-term nature of the refugee situation and the need for long-term planning (International Crisis Group, 2014; UNICEF, 2013b). UNICEF's *A Lost Generation?* recommends "a focus on systems-building and strengthening national capacity, so countries are equipped to meet the longer term needs of the younger generation in the face of challenging circumstances" (UNICEF, 2013b, p. 5). Interviewees said:

- "At the beginning, donors wanted to deal with this in a short term way, with temporary structures. Now it is becoming a lengthy problem and we need better solutions."
- "A major gap is not having a long term policy for handling them. The thinking is dealing with the humanitarian impact here and there. The long-term impact is not on the table."
- "The way we are doing things on the humanitarian side is not working. There has to be a give and take between the humanitarian issue of getting kids into school, versus long term social cohesion issues."
- "Everyone knows that they will be there for 30 years. Everyone knows it, but people are not addressing it."

Governments bear primary long-term responsibility for providing formal education. Given the crisis in access to formal education described in Chapter Two, and the need for school buildings and other infrastructure to reduce the access problem, governments need significant investment from donors to ensure that they can meet their responsibilities. UNHCR acknowledged that the governments have been the largest providers of human and financial resources in response to the crisis (3RP, 2015c). Indeed, accepting Syrians into the public education system has increased operating and capital expenses in serving the refugees' education and needs (Dhillon and Yousef, 2009; Dinçer et al., 2013; Idiz, 2014; International Rescue Committee, 2013; Kirişci, 2014; MOPIC, 2015; Rotberg, 2009).

The costs of adding Syrian children to Lebanese and Jordanian schools without additional outside financial support are unsustainable. The Lebanese and Jordanian governments are taking loans to cover the deficits. For example, Jordan took a $150 million World Bank loan in 2013 to cover deficits in health and education (Yukhananov, 2013). In Lebanon, MEHE's budget is in deficit. According to MEHE, the government of Lebanon is paying for all costs of formal education for the refugees except for parental registration fees, which UN agencies pay. MEHE's low budget also has meant a shortage of equipment, data, and training for staff in managing programs.

In response to growing appreciation for these issues, the 2015 3RP signified a paradigm shift for the UN. It calls for a "new aid architecture," involving development priorities as well as humanitarian priorities. It explains, "traditional humanitarian assistance is no longer enough, especially given that an end to the crisis is not imminent" (3RP, 2015c, pp. 4–5). The 3RP is a "first" for the UN, as it combines humanitarian and development capacities, innovation, and resources (3RP, 2015c). Education represents 10 percent of the $4.5 billion funding request from donors for 2015. The 3RP (2015c, p. 16) recognized the need for more development funds to go directly to host governments in education in these sectors, concluding,

> Although some development funds for education and child protection have been made available to host countries under the No Lost Generation initiative, more support is needed to strengthen national systems and quality of services.

New initiatives are included in the 3RP for transportation, infrastructure rehabilitation and improvements, teacher training, and working within national policy frameworks for certifications. Most funding is still for partners; only 22 percent of the budget request is slated for governments.

In the 2015 3RP, budgets are designated as supporting either refugees or resilience (the host countries' longer-term capabilities). While not an "apples to apples" comparison with Figure 3.1, in which budgets are broken down by organization type, Figure 3.2 shows budget allocations per country by refugee and resilience/stabilization responses, and it is indicative of the shift in thinking toward the longer term (MOPIC, 2015; 3RP, 2015d; 3RP, 2015e). However, in many cases, the 3RP does not specify how much of these budgets go to which entities—governments, UN agencies, or NGOs.

For Lebanon, the 2015 3RP requested budget is $264 million, of which $68 million goes toward resilience, including education services. For Jordan, the majority of the budget request goes toward resil-

Figure 3.2
Education Budget Requests for the 2015 Refugee and Resilience Response Plan

SOURCE: MOPIC, 2015; 3RP, 2015d; 3RP, 2015e.
RAND RR859-3.2

ience, with $178 million out of $257 million. (The total 3RP [2015a] budget request for all sectors in Jordan is $3 billion, of which $1.1 billion is direct budget support.) Similarly, for Turkey, the refugee budget request is $47 million, with the resilience budget at $13 million.

Jordan's 3RP noted that the total cost per Syrian student in a Jordanian public school is $1,544; with 125,000 Syrians in public schools, this means that the 2015 cost of Syrians in public schools is $193 million. In Lebanon, costs to date have been $600 per refugee child per year in the second shifts, although the World Bank estimates that the cost of educating a Lebanese child in a public school is $2,000. MEHE's *Reaching All Children with Education in Lebanon* document (2014b) estimates the need for $600 million to reach 500,000 Syrian refugee children over the next three years.[2]

Each country faces particular resource challenges. For example, Syrian schools in Turkey face particular challenges of unsustainability. Financing for both the informal Syrian schools and the UNICEF schools relies on international donors, the Syrian diaspora, NGOs, and the volunteerism of Syrian teachers. Teachers in these schools are also Syrian refugees, and Turkish law prohibited them from receiving salaries at the time of data collection. Not having the budgetary means to pay the teachers of the Syrian students is a long-term problem. Basing compensation of teachers of several hundred thousand children on volunteerism is not a sustainable solution, as teachers need the means to support themselves. Quality cannot be adequate without professionalization of teachers with sustainable salaries.

Recognizing that the Syrians may remain for the medium term is politically difficult for the host countries. They are coping with pressures from their own societies as the crisis intrudes on public services (such as education), the labor market, the housing market, internal stability, and more. However, planning should still take these time frames into account.

---

[2]   The difference between the World Bank calculation and Lebanon's MEHE calculation is likely due to the inputs counted as part of the cost calculation.

Information for Decisionmakers and Refugees

There are a number of important information sources for education of Syrian refugees in Jordan, Lebanon, and Turkey: the UNHCR information portal; surveys and studies sponsored by UN agencies; government databases, surveys, and planning documents; and household surveys of refugees in host communities and camps. At the same time, both interviewees and the documents related to refugee education concluded that needed information to support education of the refugees is lacking. Interviewees described data as "hit or miss," "scattered," "not aggregated," "not available," "fragmented," "a challenge," "not in real time," "not reliable," "not compatible," "sensitive," and "dangerous." An INEE report also noted problems of "insufficient data and evidence to inform educational response" (2014, p. 10). Characteristics of available information for decisionmakers, based on the interviews with stakeholders, are described here.

Government electronic databases are vital for education planning. Turkey has an Education Management Information System (EMIS), and Jordan is in the process of developing one. UNICEF and Turkey's MONE are working together to develop a parallel EMIS for Syrian students; this could eventually be incorporated into Turkey's. Lebanon does not have an EMIS; its MEHE relies on paper forms, fax, and Excel spreadsheets. Interviewees noted a need for EMISs to have the capability to track individual children throughout the education system and refugee response programs, as well as the ability for partners to report in—one interviewee described this as a need for "a bar code of a kid."

Compatible information was cited as a widespread issue. Interviewees across countries said that there are multiple, uncoordinated data platforms within each country, with a lack of shared information. In Lebanon, MEHE collects data from the schools. UNHCR collects data from refugee registration; children who are not registered with UNHCR are not counted. NGOs collect data, and some data are reported to a database for donors, but not to the community working in Lebanon. Interviewees said that MEHE, UNHCR, and NGOs report differing statistics. Other data collectors in Lebanon are the Center for Educational Research and Development, the Lebanese army, and UNICEF. In Turkey, there are multiple collectors of refugee data, including AFAD, the foreign police, the Directorate of Migration Management, UNHCR, and NGOs. Each has its own data system, incompatible with the others. There are also different data systems in different provinces of Turkey. In Jordan, UNHCR and the MOI collect refugee registration data, including biometrics. UNHCR collects data from refugees registering at the border, and the MOI collects information inside Jordan. Jordan's MOE collects information from schools. Save the Children collected considerable data during an outreach campaign. But none of this information is systematically shared. One interviewee called for a mapping of available data among various sources.

Government technical capabilities are very important for managing the additional refugees in the education system, as well as for managing education for citizens. Interviewees said that gathering data in this environment is very challenging because the policy and bureaucratic infrastructure is weak and because governments lack not only basic technology but also enough people with needed technological and statistical skills. In Lebanon, interviewees noted that MEHE staff lack computers to manage information, and schools also do not have computers. In Jordan, the MOE has a Technology Center for Education and Data, and MOPIC is developing the Royal National Geographic Center as a project between the government and the Jordanian army. MOPIC is incorporating assistance from the Department of Statistics in mapping public services, hospitals, clinics, schools, and population distribution. In 2015, the housing and population census, conducted once every ten years, will be taken. In Turkey, interviewees said that the government has been reticent to accept technical support.

Data sensitivity is another concern; information about the refugees, including in educational records, can have political, social, demographic, and security implications. One interviewee in Lebanon stated that, "Data about population is very dangerous, in particular education." With its "confessional" system of government, which mixes religion and politics, the balance there is delicate among Christians,

Sunnis, Shiites, and Druze, numbers of additional people, and their sectarian affiliations. Turkey is hesitant to share data, as it is concerned about the whereabouts of refugees and what this means for demographic balances in its unstable border regions. Interviewees said that a mapping process between MONE and UNICEF to determine where the Syrian students are to inform school planning was "on again, off again," as the government of Turkey seems concerned about the implications of the data. Indeed, Turkey's Ministry of Interior enacted new regulations restricting research and data collection about the refugees in Turkey (Kayaoğlu, 2015). Further, refugees in all three countries are themselves afraid, and sometimes hesitant to register as refugees or share information about themselves.

Unavailability of information hinders planning and decision-making. For those with responsibility for providing education, information is often not available. While data are more accurate in the camps, interviewees complained that data from host communities are sorely lacking and unreliable in general, as there is lack of knowledge about where refugees are. With many refugees not registered, it is difficult to collect data in cases where the locations of refugees are not known. Interviewees noted a range of needed information, including the number of students, their locations, the number of open spaces in schools, the characteristics of students who are out of school, barriers to attendance, attendance rates, school records, student needs, length of time a student has been out of school, quality indicators, information on the community schools, needs of host community schools with refugees, classroom conditions, school infrastructure needs, teachers' needs in dealing with classrooms with refugees, and more. An assessment in Lebanon called for additional data describing the type of education that children were receiving, information on private or non-formal community schools, absorptive capacity of schools, profiles of out-of-school children, and impacts on education within the host community (UNHCR, 2014b).

Standardized indicators are also lacking in many cases because there are not standard approaches to defining and using information across countries or within countries. For example, different entities within and across countries are using inconsistent definitions of "school-age child" (varying from ages 3–18 to 6–15). In Lebanon, UNHCR defines school-age children as between the ages of 3 and 18, while UNICEF does not include children in secondary school. On the other hand, Lebanon's MEHE defines school-age children as 6–15, the age of compulsory education in Lebanon. The application of different definitions can result in numbers that differ by tens of thousands, complicating budgeting and planning. Another example is differing definitions of "nonformal education" (meaning children in alternative degree programs Jordan, children in the Syrian community schools in Turkey, or children taught at home or by the community in Lebanon). Having different definitions of concepts that are central to budgets and management complicates analysis of the extent of the access crisis.

Information for refugees is important as well. According to interviewees, refugees often do not know what rights they have regarding public services, such as education, or how to go about accessing them. Websites that explain such rights to the refugees in Arabic, or even paper information sheets, are not widely used or visible. However, by many accounts, the refugees often have smartphones with data plans and Internet access, so there may be missed opportunities for information-sharing.[3] In addition, refugees themselves are using social media and Facebook to organize—for example, in hiring teachers for the community schools in Turkey. Interviewees noted repeatedly that this refugee crisis is different from others, as refugees have higher levels of technology skills and access. While there are a number of efforts to start, for example, health fact sheets or develop information apps, systematic and up-to-date information for the refugees is lacking. Apps or websites that describe services, locations, rights, points of contact, and other information would be useful.

---

[3] There are efforts to bring information on services to refugees through technology such as smart-phone applications. One example is Digital Humanitarian Network, a network of technology and humanitarian-focused organizations that developed a phone application to provide information to refugees about local area services. According to the website, this application was developed at the request of UNHCR. For more information see PeaceGeeks (undated).

Policy Considerations

Establishing education for the children among Syria's 4 million refugees in a timely way is a complex management task requiring both short- and long-term thinking and evidence upon which to base decisions. We recommend the following in support of management of refugee education.

Include longer-term development planning in addition to humanitarian responses. Four years into the crisis, with no end likely in the near future, planning needs to include a development response in addition to a humanitarian response, meaning focusing on sustainable solutions to providing formal education for larger numbers of refugees (provided by governments or other entities). The need for this shift was recognized in the 2015 3RP and incorporated into planning. There are planning, resource, and management implications, with a need for resources to flow to development actors and governments, as well as to humanitarian agencies. This requires a regional rethinking of the refugee response, with prioritization of resources to support host-country institutions so that they can manage the situation into the future as emergency efforts and funds lessen over time. This also means shifting resources to host communities that lie outside the camps in addition to camps themselves, as the host communities are where the vast majority of refugees are located and where they are likely to integrate over the long term.

Invest in building capacity for governments to manage the crisis into the future. Governments need improved management systems to support increased responsibilities with respect to refugee education. A development response involves greater resourcing and capacity-building of national education ministries, or alternative systems with quality standards and monitoring, to leave countries with systems that can be managed for the refugees over time. For example, this additional investment in schools should support building infrastructure, data systems, and teacher training at the national level. Large amounts of aid funding is coming in, although it is well below what is requested; some interviewees mentioned hesitation of donors to provide direct bilateral funding because of a lack of accountability systems in government. Development of accountability systems for financial flows could ameliorate this. In addition, other approaches, such as hiring staff with international experience in international education, could prove useful.

Prioritize funding to support medium-term formal education. With formal certified education as the end goal of the education response, it is not clear from the response plans how decisions about budget allocation have been made. In particular, in Jordan and Lebanon, the governments are providing formal education, while in Turkey, UNICEF and the Syrians themselves have started schools. Yet UN-led refugee response budget requests have largely been for the international community. Given that the situation is transitioning to a longer-term effort, prioritization of the budgets to support the basics of education (buildings and teacher salaries), as well as longer-term commitments by donors (instead of current short-term commitments) would be a useful step.

Enhance data and information in support of managing refugee education. There is a lack of information about education that is needed to support decisionmaking, budgetary planning, school infrastructure development, problem solving for access to education, and awareness among refugees. There are several ways such information may be improved. These include:

- developing a targeted and consistent set of access, quality, and protection indicators
- collecting data to support these indicators
- creating or building upon data management systems to incorporate the refugees
- enabling multiple actors dealing with refugee children to contribute to data systems
- providing electronic information to refugees.

Improve effectiveness and efficiency of the refugee education response with creative use of technology. The UNHCR 2012 assessment of its efforts to help refugees in the host communities specifically points to the need for innovative technology such as websites, mobile-messaging, and tools for increased engagement with local actors (Morand et al., 2013). In addition, UNHCR's *2012–2016 Education Strategy* (2012) calls for innovative use of technology as one of its four "strategic approaches" to expand education opportunities and outcomes for refugees. Currently, there are a number of initiatives under way or in the exploration phase to leverage technology in the provision of education. For example, one initiative under way is an online version of the Syrian curriculum under development at the UN. Technology can also be leveraged effectively to collect data and monitor progress on achieving student learning objectives. During field interviews, a number of organizations expressed interest in enabling EMISs to take into account information particular to the refugee situation, and to incorporate new data-collection methods, such as surveys of refugees and teachers administered via mobile phones. This would allow regular collection of data that would help in understanding support needs, using a device that is readily accessible to most people. Because of their accessibility, mobile phones can be effective tools in disseminating information or for outreach to deliver services to refugees.

CHAPTER FOUR

Society

The altered demographics in host countries from the presence of the refugees presents significant challenges to Syrian and host-country societies. Several of these challenges relate to education, including how children are integrated into schools and classrooms; how they are prepared for the future through certification; how parents' inability to earn a livelihood promotes child labor or early marriage, precluding education; and how schools and teachers manage the psychosocial needs of refugee children. In this chapter, we argue the need for a deliberative decisionmaking process on whether and how to integrate Syrian children with citizens, with considerations for social cohesion; a regional approach to Syrian education certification; labor-market policies to enable livelihoods and reduce the need for child labor; and psychosocial programming for schools, with training for teachers.

Structure of Refugee Education and Considerations for Social Cohesion

While all three countries allow refugees to attend national public schools, Syrian children in each country are still separated in education from citizens to an extent. There are seven models of education for the refugees. The first model is integration into public school classrooms with citizens. The other six models separate Syrians from citizens: refugee schools in camps, second shifts for refugees in public schools, community schools established by Syrian refugees, UNICEF schools outside of camps (only in Turkey, established for the 2014–

2015 school year), alternative educational programming, and education in by religious groups. Figure 4.1 shows the distribution in the 2013–2014 school year. It includes four of the seven models, as the UNICEF schools outside of camps in Turkey had not opened, and as there is no available comparative data on the alternative educational programming or education by religious groups.

In Jordan in the 2013–2014 school year, there were 120,000 Syrian students enrolled in Jordanian schools—65,000 mixed into Jordanian schools, 35,000 in Syrian-only second shifts, and 20,000 in the camps (MOE, 2014). In Jordan, interviewees said that community schools were not playing a major role in education.

In Lebanon in the 2013–2014 school year, there were 58,000 Syrian children mixed into Lebanese classrooms and 30,000 in Syrian-only second shifts (MEHE, 2014a). In Lebanon, interviewees noted that there are also community schools established by the Syrians themselves, but that there are no data on these schools. Lebanon's MEHE has indicated willingness to open Syrian-only second shifts for about

Figure 4.1
Syrian Students Enrolled in Four Models of Classrooms in 2013–2014

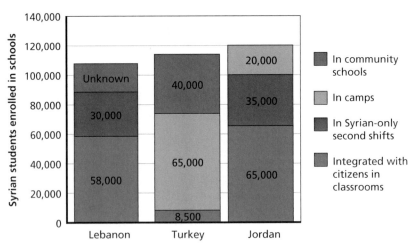

SOURCE: Kolcu, 2014; MEHE, 2014a; MOE, 2014; UNHCR, 2014g.

RAND RR859-4.1

100,000 children in the 2015–2016 school year if donor funding is sufficient.

In Turkey, a small number of Syrian children (8,500) attended Turkish public schools in 2013–2014 (UNHCR, 2014g). In the camps, 65,000 Syrian children attended school (Kolcu, 2014). As there has been an education vacuum in Turkey, Syrian communities in many areas have set up community schools with funding from a variety of sources: Turkish municipalities, NGOs, Syrian opposition, or the Syrian diaspora. Although there is no reliable data on these schools, interviewees estimated that 25,000 to 40,000 Syrian students attended at least 60 such schools in the 2013–2014 school year. Interviewees noted plans in the future for Turkey's MONE to survey the community schools. UNICEF also built 40 prefabricated schools in areas of Turkey with high concentrations of refugees. They are not included here in the figure for the 2013–2014 school year.

Therefore, in the 2013–2014 school year in Jordan,[1] 54 percent of the known numbers of Syrian children enrolled in formal education were in classrooms with Jordanian children, 46 percent were in separate schools. In Lebanon, 66 percent of enrolled Syrian students were in classrooms with Lebanese children, with the remaining 34 percent in separate classes. In Turkey, 7 percent of Syrian students were in classrooms with Turkish children, the remaining 93 percent were in separate Syrian schools. As Syrian-only second shifts become an expanded model, the numbers of Syrian children educated separately will increase.

In the short term, there are compelling reasons for this separation of the Syrians and host-country citizens in education. There are significant space constraints; it is logistically challenging to expand educational programming so quickly; new schools and shifts are starting in areas with large concentrations of Syrians; it is challenging for teachers to integrate Syrian students into new curricula; in some cases, there are

---

[1] These numbers were the most recent comparative numbers available to this study. While percentages might have shifted to an extent in the 2014–2015 school year, the educational models are still the same, with a large percentage of Syrian children educated separately from host-country children.

language barriers; and some students who have been out of school for significant periods and have been traumatized may need special circumstances and also may slow instruction or affect the classroom environment for citizens. Furthermore, many citizens of these countries feel resentment toward the large number of new students and may feel inundated with large numbers of refugees in classrooms.

There are additional particular considerations in each country. In Turkey, there is a desire to continue with Arabic-language instruction as provided in the Syrian community schools, UNICEF schools, or camps because native-language education is important (INEE, 2010). One study in Jordan found that 61 percent of Jordanians and 44 percent of Syrians reported that access to education was causing tension in their community, and that mixed classes, poor management of educational services, overcrowded schools, school-based violence, discrimination between Jordanian and Syrian students, and disagreement over curricula contributed to the tension (REACH, 2014b). In Lebanon, the numbers of Syrian school-age children outnumber the Lebanese children enrolled in public schools. Furthermore, while Turkey and Jordan and the Syrians are all largely Sunni, Lebanon has a particularly delicate balance of religious identities that needs to be considered. Clearly, some of these demographic issues are about more-comprehensive and bigger societal and political issues than just education.

However, there are also longer-term risks to separately educating different groups of children residing in the same communities. Social psychologists have examined this issue closely in other contexts, and while there is broad acknowledgement of the challenges presented by diversity, scholarship continues to heavily favor integrated education. Integrated education seems to bear particular importance on overall societal health and cohesion; there is a great deal of evidence that, under the right conditions, intergroup contact facilitates reduction of prejudice and facilitates more harmonious intergroup relations (Pettigrew and Tropp, 2006; Van Laar, Levin, and Sidanius, 2008), whereas segregation often leads to polarization, stereotyping, social isolation, and diminished ability to adapt to a diverse society (Ouseley, 2001). In particular, there are risks of reduced social cohesion over time in countries that already have fragile relations between ethnic and religious groups. Some scholars have argued that Lebanon's private school system, in which 70 percent of Lebanese children attend private schools separated by ethnicity, religion, or social class, have contributed to ongoing sectarian tensions (Euro-Trends, 2009, p. 23). In post-conflict settings—such as Northern Ireland, with its history of violent conflict between Catholics and Protestants and where many children are educated separately according to religious affiliation—studies show that segregated education does not facilitate reconciliation, but rather contributes to group polarization (Donnelly and Hughes, 2006; Gallagher, 2004; Hughes, 2007; Hughes, 2011; Hughes et al., 2008; Niens and Cairns, 2005).

In addition, UNHCR (2011a, p. 4) provided guidance in 2011:

> Setting up parallel education services for refugees should be avoided if possible. Incorporating refugees within the national system ensures sustainability and supports peaceful co-existence of refugees within host communities both in the short and long term.

Similarly, the Norwegian Refugee Council argues that while segregation of displaced school children from host-community children may be necessary in early phases of displacement (for example, to take into account language needs, or when sheer numbers of displaced children overwhelm the public education system), integration is better in the longer term for education quality and social cohesion (Internal Displacement Monitoring Centre and Norwegian Refugee Council, 2011). UNHCR's 2011 review of global refugee education suggested integrating refugees into national education systems and working closely with ministries of education and UNICEF to benefit not only refugees but also host communities (Dryden-Peterson, 2011, p. 7). In practice, this may mean allowing flexibility in the language of instruction while still adequately preparing students in the host-country language to ensure a base level of language proficiency.

Current approaches in Lebanon, Turkey, and Jordan of separating a proportion of the Syrians from host-country nationals have the potential to undermine social cohesion in the long term. As Syrians are likely to remain where they are for many years, there are risks in each country of a new population that is separated from the rest of the community, with a perception of receiving lower-quality services (Dinçer et al., 2013; Parkinson, 2014). As one interviewee said, "This parallel system of education for Syrians will reach a point in which it can't sustain itself. There is a big risk of setting a precedent for ethnic or identity-based education." In addition, there are other implications to not being educated in the host country's language, including lack of labor-market integration, reduced higher-education opportunities, societal isolation, and discrimination.

Indeed, past refugee situations have led to long-term separate education for different groups in Jordan and Lebanon. More than 65 years after the arrival of Palestinian refugees, while many Palestinians are integrated into public schools, many are still educated separately. The United Nations Relief and Works Agency for Palestine Refugees in the Near East (UNRWA) runs 172 schools in Jordan, for 122,000 Palestinian refugees (United Nations Education, Scientific and Cultural Organization, 2012). In Lebanon, UNRWA educates 32,000 Palestinians in separate schools (UNRWA, 2013). This arrangement was a political decision, agreed to by some of the Palestinians, who wanted to maintain a separate identity, and by the host countries, who feared demographic changes in their countries. These countries now risk a similar separate long-term structure for Syrians, in addition to the separate structure for the Palestinians. Separate education as set up now has the potential to continue indefinitely on the ongoing assumption that the refugees will return to Syria soon. Like the Palestinian case, deciding whether and how to integrate Syrian children into educational settings—and the implications of that decision for national identity—will pose a difficult political choice.

Turkey also faces sensitivities around treating minorities differently. With its difficult history of conflict with minorities, Turkey has invested in creating a national identity and unifying a multiethnic society through education. Turkey's Law on Unity of Education, established at the republic's founding, argues for education as a source of national solidarity, with the Turkish language as a unifying factor (Eurydice, 2011). On the other hand, the political environment following the early years of Turkey's republic also resulted in the suppression of other languages, such as Kurdish, but this policy has been modified in recent times (Cemiloglu, 2009), with the Kurdish language introduced into the curriculum in some cases per the desire of Kurdish minorities.

In sum, the risks to creating a minority that is educated in a different language and education system must be weighed against political sensitivities in the host countries about how the citizens view the rapid addition of new students, future plans for the Syrians to return to their homes or integrate into the host communities (and host communities' views on this issue), the rights of minorities to education in their native tongue, and the challenges and logistics of integrating a large,

Table 4.1
Advantages and Risks of Separate and Integrated Education for Syrian Refugees

Option	Advantages	Risks
Separate education	• May be preferable for host-country citizens in early stages of crisis, as refugee children must adapt to new circumstances, curriculum, and language • Could better serve needs of Syrian children, targeting unique education and psychosocial needs of traumatized population • May be more politically feasible for governments to argue that refugees will leave soon • May reduce tensions between communities in early stages of crisis • In Jordan and Lebanon, may be easier in the short term to help Syrian children adapt to new curriculum • May better preserve Syrian identity • In Turkey and Lebanon, will keep Arabic language proficiency for Syrians and make return to Syria easier • In Turkey and Jordan, ensures that children in refugee camps attend school • May be logistically expedient in setting up new schools and shifts	• May provide lower-quality education for Syrian minority if quality in the additional shifts and schools is not regulated • May exacerbate tensions between Syrians and host-country nationals in the long term by creating a perception of lower-quality education for Syrians • Risks having a traumatized minority isolated from the rest of society • Risks strengthening religious, ethnic, and national identities and divisions • In Turkey, a parallel school system may be unsustainable if it is not accredited, not financed, and lacks pathways to university, vocational education, or employment

Table 4.1—Continued

Option	Advantages	Risks
Integrated education	• May promote social cohesion and integrated identities in the long term • Will help Syrian students transition to work or further education in host country • May provide a sense of fairness to Syrians in host countries • May offer higher-quality education than separate education • May reduce risks of future instability by not promoting identity-based education • May be more sustainable in the long run than a parallel education system for the Syrians managed and financed by the international community • Would offer certified pathways for further education or employment	• Could exacerbate tensions between Syrians and citizens who resent crowded classes • May be harder for Syrians in Turkey to reintegrate into employment and education upon return to Syria • The numbers of Syrians in Lebanon in comparison with Lebanese in public schools could have big implications on structure of school system • May weaken Syrian identity • Could be viewed in the short term as lower quality for the Syrians while they adapt to language changes • Reduces native-language education • May place pressures on the poorest of the host-country nationals • In the short term, may slow educational instruction as students from a different curriculum are integrated • Could be logistically complicated to integrate in the short term • Could burden schools with large class sizes, finding qualified teachers, diversity of student needs, language challenges

new population. Balancing these many issues will be complex, and may require trade-offs. Table 4.1 describes the advantages and risks of separate and integrated education.

Issues of Certification

Interviewees, particularly in Turkey, raised issues of education certification (for example, obtaining a ninth-grade diploma, secondary-school diploma, or tertiary diploma) as one of the most important challenges to address, as certification is key to longer-term integration into education and labor markets in both Syria and the host countries. Education needs to provide refugees with the skills and qualifications for two main scenarios: integration into the host country or return to Syria (a small percentage will resettle in a third country). Syrian children need an education with pathways leading to vocational education, employment, or higher education both in Syria and their new host country at the same time; certification enables these pathways.

Certification of studies is a challenge that is not unique to the education of Syrian refugees. It is also a challenge in other refugee situations, in which displaced people may not have ready access to certification in their home country or in the host country. Approaches to recognizing education for refugees in other circumstances have included finding ways to provide access examinations from their home countries, provide access to host-country examinations, or set up certification boards for a particular refugee crisis (Dryden-Peterson, 2011; Kirk, 2009).

In Turkey, there are multiple curricula used with Syrian children. First, some community schools use the Syrian national curriculum, but they are not accredited and cannot lead to certification. Second, as Turkey is hosting the Syrian opposition government (with a parallel Syrian Ministry of Education in Gaziantep, Turkey), opposition figures developed the "Syrian Adapted Curriculum," based on the Syrian curriculum but modified in terms of political messages and pedagogy. The UNICEF schools in the refugee camps and in host communities have implemented the Syrian Adapted Curriculum. However, interviewees noted that this curriculum is not accredited or recognized elsewhere. It is also politically charged, and many parents hesitate to send their children to schools using it, concerned that such certification (associated with the opposition) could mean retribution upon return to Syria. Since choice of which Syrian curriculum to use is controversial, some community schools are using the Libyan curriculum. Interviewees gave varying reasons for this: The Libyan curriculum is in Arabic; it is recognized by Turkish higher-education institutions and employers; and the government of Libya has agreed to allow Syrian children to take their exams and receive certifications. This facilitates Syrian refugee students' prospects for higher education and jobs while averting the political concerns associated with the Syrian curriculum options. This fragmented set of curricula and examinations in Turkey is not conducive to a consistent, high-quality set of pathways to education and the labor market for Syrians and requires a more coherent plan.

In Jordan and Lebanon, there are different opportunities and challenges. Jordan, Lebanon, and Syria have mutual recognition of each other's curricula and certifications. In some cases, the Jordanian MOE is offering Syrian certification exams in addition to the Jordanian secondary-school exit exam (*Tawjihi*). In Lebanon, interviewees described problems in enabling Syrians to take the Lebanese secondary-school exit exam, as it requires identification papers (which many Syrians lack), and there is concern about fraud if Syrians take exams without identification. Interviewees noted a need for an examination process allowing Syrian refugees to take the Syrian secondary-school exit exam. In addition, since alternative education programs are not accredited, it is not clear how certification will be handled for children in those programs; if formal alternative education programs are developed and scaled up, determining how to certify the attainment of children who have attended will be an important component.

The Relation Between Livelihoods and Access to Education

Lebanon, Jordan, and Turkey all have restrictions on Syrian refugees working (Bidinger et al., 2014; Lebanese Institute for Democracy and Human Rights, 2013; "Syrian Refugees Get to Work in Turkey," 2014; UNHCR, 2003). These countries have high unemployment rates and seek to protect their own citizens from a sudden influx of competing workers; governments and citizens are concerned with how the addition of the Syrians will affect unemployment overall. For example, a World Bank report found that the arrival of the Syrians in Lebanon doubled the unemployment rate there, with particular impact on unskilled youth (World Bank, 2013). The Turkish Statistical Institute announced that the refugees' presence has led to an in increase in unemployment of 0.3 percent, or 251,000 Turks (Cetingulec, 2014). Yet a longer-term solution to the employment of Syrians is vital. Syrians need to be able to support themselves and their families, as there is not enough international aid to support everyone who is displaced now, much less everyone who will be in the future. If Syrians could work, they could also be taxed to support needed social services, such as education. Many Syrian adults who cannot work legally find low-wage jobs in the informal labor market with the risk of exploitation. Syrians working at low wages illegally also create the potential to drive down wages in the formal labor market for citizens. For survival and supplemental income, families rely on children entering the labor market or on girls marrying early—both of which remove educational opportunities. A UNHCR report (2013, p. 10) concludes:

> In both Jordan and Lebanon, children as young as seven years old are working long hours for little pay, sometimes in dangerous or exploitative conditions. While some girls are employed, notably in agriculture and domestic work, the majority of working children are boys. Sheer financial necessity is at the core of almost all cases of child labour . . . An enormous burden falls on working children's shoulders.

A survey in Lebanon found that 6.5 percent of respondents said that their children are sent to work (INEE, 2014). Another study found that 10 percent of children in Jordan were engaged in child labor (UNICEF, 2013b). Yet another found that the rate of child marriages (involving someone under the age of 18) among Syrian refugees in Jordan rose from 18 percent of total marriages in 2012 to 32 percent in 2014. Before Syria's civil war, 13 percent of marriages involved an individual under the age of 18 (UNICEF, 2014b).

The Classroom as a Protective Environment

The psychosocial state of Syrian refugee children has been severely affected by war, displacement, relocation in a new country, and continuing uncertainty and deprivation in their daily lives (UNHCR, 2014c). Many Syrian children have experienced or seen horrific events, loss, and violence; lost parents or saw homes destroyed; are traumatized and face mental health problems. Many have experienced separation from family and are worried about family members back in Syria. Going to school is difficult—refugee children have fallen behind academically, face bullying, go to school hungry, and have difficulty concentrating (UNHCR, 2013, p. 15). This environment has produced reported feelings of fear, sadness, anger, worry, restlessness, and other negative emotional manifestations in refugee children. In one survey, 74 percent of the children had experienced the death of somebody they cared strongly about, and 50 percent had been exposed to six or more traumatic events. About 60 percent had symptoms of depression, 45 percent has posttraumatic stress disorder, 22 percent showed aggression, and 65 percent displayed psychosomatic symptoms to a degree that seriously reduced the child's level of functioning. Some children experienced two or more of these mental health problems (Özer, Şirin, and Oppedal, 2013). Child refugees also face myriad challenges, including but not limited to violence (domestic, family, gender-based), child labor, fear of sexual violence, and early marriage (Song, 2013, p. 4).

An entire generation of Syrian children is developing a world outlook shaped by exposure to the violence they have witnessed or directly experienced; therefore, these children have particular needs for psychosocial support. The UNICEF reports *Shattered Lives* (2013a, p. 16) and *No Lost Generation* (2014a) address child protection, gender-based violence, mental health and psychosocial support, and other issues faced by refugees, and they offer recommendations to the international communities involved in this work, including seeking ways for classrooms to provide a protective environment.

In addition, there are significant pressures placed on schools and teachers with refugees in their classrooms, according to interviewees. Schools do not have systems in place to deal with the needs of traumatized students, such as counseling and referral systems. Teachers must adapt to teaching large classes containing students with special needs, including many with mental health or concentration issues linked to their traumatic experiences. However, what is being offered in all three countries is normal schooling, according to interviewees—approaches to education have not been adapted to the needs of children who have been displaced and traumatized. By and large, schools and teachers are not prepared to deal professionally with traumatized students who have need of psychosocial support, and there has not been sufficient time to roll out new school programs or comprehensive training to help teachers manage these challenges in the classroom. There are smaller programs for teacher training, and in Jordan, there has been focus on training newly hired teachers in classroom management and dealing with traumatized students. Psychosocial programs in schools are important for the long term; school systems have not yet had time to adapt to these circumstances.

Policy Considerations

Refugee education is intertwined with societal considerations, and we describe some of these here: integration or separation of refugees and citizens, certification as a path to future education or the labor market, the importance of livelihoods for adults to reduce the need for child labor in place of education, and school psychosocial programs and teacher training. Here, we offer recommendations to address these issues.

Weigh the advantages and disadvantages of integration or separation of Syrians within public schools, and create a deliberative strategy to address this question. In ramping up capacity of education systems to accommodate the refugees, large proportions of refugees are attending school separated from citizens. There are compelling reasons for this in the short term, including logistics of expanding school spaces quickly, the needs of the Syrians, and relations with host communities. In the longer term, however, if the Syrians stay, separating them in a parallel education system may pose significant risks to social cohesion in society.

A key risk is that these circumstances, developed as a quick response to need, could evolve into a de facto long-term system, similar to what happened with the Palestinians, without ever stepping back and analyzing goals, feasibility, or risks at a regional level for Syrian education. Regardless of decisions made now, governments and international organizations should undertake a decisionmaking process, with deliberative choices about the structure of the education system at key junctures. There are complex considerations and trade-offs among integration of students, the politics of identity, political tensions, quality of education, government capacity, logistical feasibility, intergroup social cohesion, speed, and the structures of the countries' education systems. There is a tension among all of these considerations, and it may not be possible to find a single solution that meets all objectives. That said, this issue calls for the creation of a strategy with a phased plan featuring policies that have been set deliberatively, not reactively. As discussed in Chapter One, there is need for planning to be based on both short-term and longer-term scenarios.

Because of the capacity of the governments and other considerations, formalized, certified, full-time alternative educational programs and approaches may need to be developed for the Syrians, as discussed in Chapter Two. These alternative approaches should also be integrated into a comprehensive strategic approach.

There are different considerations in each country for this issue. In Turkey, integration into Turkish-language public classrooms may be seen as a tacit acknowledgment that the Syrians could remain for a while. There, if an integrated approach is chosen later, younger Syrian children could be integrated over time into Turkish-language classrooms because of greater ease of adapting to language changes. If Syrian children are mixed into Turkey's public schools, the strategy for doing so should give special consideration to Arabic-language preservation for the Syrians so that they do not lose their mother tongue. This could mean additional classes offered in Arabic.

Because of the size of the refugee population in comparison with Lebanon's confessional system that balances ethnic identities, it may not be logistically or politically feasible or desirable to integrate Syrians into Lebanese classrooms in the short term. In Jordan, there may be additional room for integration of the Syrians, as the language is the same and there are fewer Syrians proportionally in Jordan than in Lebanon. However, Jordan's border regions, where many of the Syrians are, face the same issue as in Lebanon, with more Syrians than Jordanians in need of education. In Jordan and Lebanon, a parallel system of education for the Syrians in the longer term would add to structures of identity-based education, entrenching systems of separating children by social class, religion, ethnicity, and nationality. Currently, while some Syrians are being absorbed in public education systems, an ad hoc parallel system of education is being formed, not as part of an intentional strategy, but because of the need for a fast response to educational needs. If integration is a long-term goal in Lebanon and Jordan, then teachers and children from the first and second shifts could be mixed.

Coordinate curriculum standards and certification exams on a regional level as a strategy to prepare Syrian students for two scenarios: returning to life in Syria and integrating into the host countries. First, we suggest a comparison of the curriculum standards (or implied curriculum standards, if written standards do not exist) of the Syrian curriculum with the Turkish, Jordanian, Lebanese, and Syrian Adapted Curriculum. Where the Syrian curriculum standards are not included or met in the other curricula, we suggest creation of a system of additional books or supports that would enable Syrian students to sit for exams in both their host country and in Syria. Second, because the Syrian exams to receive diplomas or to progress from one level to the next are either not available in the host countries or difficult to access, we suggest offering a neutral, internationally hosted set of Syrian exams in the host countries (for example, through the UN) that Syrian students could take to obtain certification. Finally, if alternative formal education programs are developed, this would require an approach to providing certification for children in these programs.

Develop a plan to enable Syrian employment, with consideration for mitigating the effects on the local labor market. A lack of legal ability for Syrian parents to work and support their families creates circumstances and incentives for Syrian refugee child labor, precluding school attendance. An evidence-based approach to Syrian employment is needed, mitigating the potentially harmful effects that the influx is having on host-country workers, while giving Syrians the capability to support themselves and their children. Host countries are generally not addressing this issue directly, and this is not a sustainable long-term strategy. In addition, Syrian refugees bring skills, capabilities, and contribution to the economies in which they reside. Some start businesses. They contribute labor, and thus employers enjoy the benefits of the increased labor supply. Their labor could be taxed, which would help support the social services that they need, such as education. A labor market study assessing the benefits that the refugees can bring, along with analysis of how to further enable these contributions, would inform an appropriate policy response.

Develop programs at the national scale to better prepare schools and teachers to address the psychosocial needs of refugee students. Schools need structured programs to meet the psychosocial needs of students, and teachers need training in dealing with traumatized students, managing classrooms with students of multiple levels, and teaching in large classrooms. While it is beyond the scope of this report to fully assess the evidence base for systems and training for psychosocial support, ways of adapting schooling to needs of refugees could include, for example, shorter lessons, more physical activity, flexible schedules, additional strategies to address bullying, and treating classes as a multigrade environment. This could also include creating supportive structures in schools, such as new counseling programs, counselors, new approaches to identification and referral for students with psychosocial needs, or teaching materials or textbooks that help in this new classroom setting. Teachers in urban and rural areas with high concentrations of refugees could be trained on a larger scale in managing psychosocial needs, and teacher colleges could add courses so that new graduates have these skills.

CHAPTER FIVE

Quality

Accommodating the education needs of a large number of refugees has posed challenges to the quality of education, for both citizens and refugees, as resources are strained, classrooms become more crowded, and public education systems struggle to keep up. This chapter examines the issues surrounding the quality of education for refugees. It makes three recommendations: ensure adequate instructional time when creating double shifts; provide monitoring and support for double shifts and community schools established for Syrians, and continue investment in development of host country school systems so that the quality of education does not regress.

Quality of Education for Refugees

Interviewees expressed concerns about the quality of education offered to refugees, in particular in the second-shift schools in Jordan and Lebanon and in the community schools in Turkey. Considerations with quality include teacher experience and compensation, instructional time, monitoring and support, and alternative education programs.

Teacher experience is variable. To staff additional shifts in schools, the Jordanian MOE and Lebanese MEHE have hired new teachers. Finding enough people in the Jordanian and Lebanese labor forces to hire as teachers has not been a problem, as these countries have a large number of unemployed university graduates searching for work. However, the teachers are mainly new hires who lack experience and are coping with challenging classroom situations. In Jordan, many new teachers are also paid at a lower rate than teachers hired through the typical civil service process. Interviewees noted concerns about the abilities of this new teacher cohort to deal with the challenges of the classrooms and to deliver education at the desired quality.

Syrian refugees themselves cannot be employed as teachers in Lebanon or Jordan due to labor laws that restrict public-sector jobs (such as teaching) to citizens. Some Syrian refugees volunteer in outreach to increase enrollment; some in Jordan serve as teaching assistants in camp classrooms; and some teach in informal education programs offered by NGOs. Interviewees said that Syrians serving as assistant teachers in the camps in Jordan contributed to smoothing the transition of those Syrian children to the new curriculum and mediating between the children and new Jordanian teachers struggling with large classes.

In Turkey, teachers staffing the community schools and UNICEF schools are Syrian refugees themselves who cannot be paid for their work as teachers. Most are working as "volunteers." Some are receiving small "incentives" in the form of payment, but the amounts vary and are far from what would be considered a living wage in Turkey. This lack of payment is not sustainable. These schools are not publicly funded, Syrian parents cannot afford to pay, and there is no legal mechanism that would allow the Syrian teachers to work for a salary. If the Syrian teachers cannot receive salaries, many of them will have to seek other employment to survive. For example, one Syrian principal in Turkey interviewed for this study said he was volunteering his time as the school principal, while his school-age son worked in the services sector to support the family. For the Syrian community schools in Turkey to continue operating, a mechanism must be developed to compensate teachers.

Instructional time and crowding affect educational quality. An important outcome of creating double-shift schools has been the reduced instructional time for all students in these schools. Jordanian schools typically operate from 8 a.m. until 2 p.m. (six hours), and schools operating on shifts now have a morning session for Jordanians and an afternoon session for Syrians, with 4.5 or 5 hours of time per shift. UNICEF schools in Turkey similarly are operating in double shifts. This has meant that many schools fall significantly short of the

OECD average of 800 instructional hours per year (OECD, 2009). The reduced instructional time for children in these schools impacts quality of schooling. UNICEF's *A Lost Generation?* concludes, "Double-shifting in overcrowded schools re-introduced to absorb Syrian students is affecting quality and derailing ongoing public education system reform" (2013b, p. 12). In addition, many schools that are not double-shifted are becoming crowded as they absorb more children in classrooms. The RRP6 (UNHCR, 2014e) concludes

> Accommodating Syrian children is placing a profound strain on fragile national education systems, causing delays in planned education reforms. Children from host communities, who are often themselves facing economic constraints, are studying in classrooms that are overcrowded and under-resourced. The efficiency of the public education system is at serious risk, with the most marginalized groups bearing a disproportionate burden.

Monitoring, support, and training need to be increased. Across the three countries, interviewees described a lack of monitoring and support—for the second-shift schools for Syrians in Lebanon and Jordan, and in the community schools in Turkey and Lebanon. Interviewees in Lebanon and Jordan said that the second shift is not administered and monitored in the same way as the first because the ministries lack capacity. In addition, in Lebanon, there is also budgetary autonomy (without monitoring) given to principals of second-shift schools, while there is not such autonomy in the first shifts; some interviewees raised concerns that lack of oversight and accountability in the budgets might lead to misappropriation of funds. Lebanon's MEHE and UN agencies acknowledged little information about the Syrian community schools operating in Lebanon. MEHE officials noted that they have no way of monitoring these schools; it is not clear which curriculum is being used, or what kind of backgrounds the instructional staff members have. In Turkey, UNICEF and MONE monitor and manage the UNICEF schools. However, there is no monitoring of quality, teacher qualifications, school buildings, curriculum, or materials in the community schools, although interviewees said MONE is making plans to bring these schools under its monitoring programs.

Interviewees relayed anecdotes of problems with quality and management within the schools.

In addition, interviewees noted the new and varied challenges that teachers with newly crowded classrooms and on second shifts face, and they called for training on handling these situations. There are a variety of NGO, UN, or university programs to provide limited training to these teachers. This training can address challenges associated with being new teachers; dealing with large classes; and helping students with needs related to the crisis, such as psychological trauma, low achievement from having missed school, and inability to concentrate in the classroom. However, interviewees raised questions about the quality, impact, and sufficiency of teacher training in addressing their actual needs.

In the alternative education programs, it is not clear how programs have fit into a coherent quality framework across the three countries; if these programs scale up, there would be need for both a quality framework and a monitoring framework for these programs.

Quality of Education for Citizens

The refugee influx is affecting the quality of education in the host countries, in Jordan and Lebanon in particular.

Beginning in 2003, Jordan implemented a systemwide effort to improve the quality of education, entitled "Education Reform for Knowledge Economy" (World Bank, undated). While Jordan has achieved near universal primary education, when it participated in the Trends in International Mathematics and Science Study (TIMSS), it scored below the TIMSS scale centerpoint among participating countries (TIMSS, 2012). Interviewees expressed concern that a student population increase of 10–20 percent would endanger progress on Jordan's goals for improving quality, including quality improvements in the curriculum, reduction of crowding in classrooms, and ending double shifts in Jordanian schools. The presence of the refugees crowds classrooms, strains school infrastructure, places pressures on teachers in classroom management, may slow down typical classroom learning because of a need to introduce a large number of students who have been out of school to a new curriculum, and reduces Jordan's budget for other quality improvements. These pressures affect Jordan's own urban vulnerable populations the most. There are concerns about Jordan's abilities to continue with its education reforms and development while dealing with these issues.

Lebanon's strategy document for addressing education of both Lebanese students and Syrian refugees, entitled *Reaching All Children with Education in Lebanon,* lays out a plan for improving education quality (MEHE, 2014b). Lebanon also participated in the international science and math tests for TIMSS in 2011, and similar to Jordan, scored below the TIMSS scale centerpoint (TIMSS, 2012). After multiple conflicts in past decades that weakened the state, Lebanon has developed a strong private school sector to fill the gaps in its public education system. Only an estimated 30 percent of Lebanese students attend public schools, with the rest educated in private schools (UNHCR, 2014b). Lebanon's public school system therefore serves 275,000 citizen children (UNICEF, 2013b); their numbers are surpassed by the estimated half-million school-age Syrian children in need of education. With the increase of children in public schools in Lebanon, there are risks to the quality of education for Lebanese nationals—including larger class sizes, teachers managing large and diverse classes, and less instructional time because of double-shifted schedules. MEHE faces capacity constraints to manage quality during the crisis; interviewees noted that MEHE lacks required equipment, such as cars, computers, photocopiers, phones, and stationary. Staff often buy their own supplies.

There is an impression among Jordanians and Lebanese that Syrians are crowding them out. There are many communities in Jordan and Lebanon with significant development challenges, and there is a perception that resources are being channeled away from their needs to meet the needs of the growing Syrian refugee communities, in education as well as other sectors. To address some of this, the Jordanian government has mandated a policy that 30 percent of all foreign aid targeted toward Syrians must be reserved for Jordanians, and some donors now require that a percentage of assistance must go to vulnerable Lebanese. Jordanians and Lebanese citizens increasingly believe that Syrian refugees are placing strain on resources, while they have received insufficient funding and support to assist with supporting these refugees (Shteiwi, Walsh, and Klassen, 2014). In fact, this underlies recent moves by the Lebanese, Jordanian, and Turkish governments to restrict previously unfettered entry of Syrians into the country.

Policy Considerations

The quality of education is a vital consideration for the long-term development needs of both refugees and host country nationals. Additional influxes of people, disruption of refugees' education, and resource constraints all threaten the quality of education. Here are a number of options that might mitigate some of the quality challenges.

Ensure adequate instructional time in first and second shift schools. Adding a second shift means reducing time spent in school each day for one or both shifts. This has meant reduced instructional time for the refugee students—and, in some cases, the host-country students—affecting the quality of education. However, double-shifted schools do not necessarily mean a reduction in the quality of education, as long as adequate instructional time is maintained and teacher quality is consistent in both shifts. Other developing countries coping with school infrastructure shortages (including South Korea, Hong Kong, Indonesia, Brazil, and Chile, for example) have still managed to promote high-quality education systems by adding school days to compensate for instructional time lost from adding a second shift. Studies suggest that students in double-shift schools can perform at the same level as students in single-shift schools, provided that there is enough instructional time, and assuming that teacher quality is similar in both shifts (Bray, 2008; Conference des Ministres de l'Education, 2003; Farrell and Schiefelbein, 1974; Fuller et al., 1999; Linden, 2001). Formal education should aim for 800 hours of instructional time per year at the primary level.

Strategically support teachers with refugees in their classrooms. There are several ways that this could be done. First, in all three countries, target additional teacher training toward teachers with refugees among their students. Additional training is needed in dealing with classes with students at multiple skill levels, traumatized students, and crowding. Second, if it is politically feasible with the longer-term teachers in Jordan and Lebanon, mix experienced and newly hired teachers in both the first and second shifts so that the second shift is not composed entirely of inexperienced teachers: As is typical practice, newly hired teachers could be mixed in with and mentored by experienced teachers. Third, the government of Turkey could coordinate with donors or the Syrian community to allow salaried payment of the Syrian teachers in the Syrian schools. Fourth, in Jordan and Lebanon, integrate Syrian teachers as teaching assistants into classrooms in the host communities, much in the way they are in the camps.

Introduce new schools and shifts into national school monitoring systems, and develop additional monitoring and support approaches appropriate to the new situations. In all three countries, additional school monitoring and support for the schools or shifts for the Syrian students is needed, in terms of ensuring standards in teacher qualifications, school buildings, or materials. Additional support and monitoring, ensuring that the schools and shifts for the Syrians are meeting host-country quality standards (or are supported toward goals of meeting those standards), would be a valuable step. This may mean integrating these shifts and schools into national school monitoring programs—and, in addition, developing new modes of training and quality-monitoring elements specific to the needs of refugee children and to the alternative educational programs that are educating those children. If alternative formal education programs are developed and scaled up, quality standards and monitoring would be an element to include in design and implementation.

Keep focused attention on the education needs of host-country nationals. Amid all of this, the needs of host-country nationals should be prioritized and addressed. Interviewees mentioned impressions across countries that the presence of the Syrian refugees is harming quality education for their own populations. The host countries have development needs and vulnerable populations of their own; international education assistance should take into account development considerations of these countries while planning for the Syrian refugees.

CHAPTER SIX

Conclusion

The Syrian refugee crisis is creating an education crisis—a lost generation of children without education across multiple countries of the Middle East. Host governments, host-country citizens, the international assistance community, and the refugees themselves have made tremendous progress in addressing refugee education needs in a short period of time, and under very difficult circumstances. The Syrian refugee children are a global responsibility, not only a responsibility of the host countries, and international donors (including traditional donors, such the United States and European Union, as well as wealthy Arab states) have a responsibility to sustain financial and other support to the refugees as well as the host countries.

At the same time, new approaches and ways of planning are needed in order to create sustainable solutions that enable Syrian children to pursue their education, help governments cope, balance the social and political considerations involved with refugee education, and ameliorate the impact on host country education. In this report, we have provided an overview of Syrian refugee education in Lebanon, Turkey, and Jordan; identified key trends and challenges; and described policy considerations intended to be of use to host governments, the international donor community, UN agencies, and NGOs. Focus is needed on access, management, society and quality to enable the education and well-being of these children into the future. These circumstances lead to a number of policy considerations, and call particularly for a coordinated strategy to increase access for the out-of-school children. The "Summary" text box summarizes the policy considerations for refugee education described in this study.

Summary of Access, Management, Society, and Quality Policy Considerations

Access
• Develop a coordinated strategy to address access for out-of-school children.
• Develop a plan to make strategic use of more available school spaces.
• Create additional shifts in public schools, with greater attention to quality.
• Develop consistent, quality formal educational alternatives.
• Analyze scope of barriers to access and develop plans to address those barriers.
• Pursue an innovative school financing and building plan.

Management
• Include longer-term development planning in addition to humanitarian responses.
• Invest in building capacity for governments to manage the crisis into the future.
• Prioritize funding to support formal education.
• Enhance data and information in support of managing refugee education.
• Improve effectiveness and efficiency of the refugee education response with creative use of technology.

Society
• Weigh the advantages and disadvantages of integration or separation of the Syrians within public schools, and create a deliberative strategy to address this question.
• Coordinate curriculum standards and certification exams on a regional level as a strategy to prepare Syrian students for two scenarios: returning to life in Syria and integrating into the host countries.
• Develop a plan to enable Syrian employment, with consideration for mitigating the effects on the local labor market.
• Develop programs at the national scale to better prepare schools and teachers to address the psychosocial needs of refugee students.

Quality
• Ensure adequate instructional time in first- and second-shift schools.
• Strategically support teachers with refugees in their classes.
• Introduce new schools and shifts into national school monitoring systems, and develop additional monitoring and support approaches appropriate to the new situations.
• Keep focused attention on the education needs of host country nationals.

Clearly, managing refugee education and implementing new initiatives is no easy task, particularly for such a large population that grew so quickly. While this study serves as a broad overview of the circumstances, challenges, and ideas for the way forward, further studies are needed to assess feasibility, prescribe optimal options, and support implementation.

Still, to provide additional perspectives on the policy considerations presented in this report, we propose a set of goals and considerations—based on the interviews, the literature, and the analysis in previous chapters—to guide further planning for managing access, quality, and social cohesion of refugee education. Some of these goals have been described in interviews and the literature; some have been assumed. Goals include cost-effectiveness, use of existing resources, management of different future scenarios, host-community relations, equity, shared responsibility, political feasibility, government capacity, benefits to host countries, quality and values, safety, sustainability, cohesive national identities, native language education, host-country language proficiency, reduction or elimination of long-term parallel education systems, integration, decisiveness and action, and deliberative strategies. Table 6.1 lays out these goals; we note that a review of the goals in the table reveals many ambitious and conflicting objectives.

While education stakeholders might debate some of these goals and how to prioritize them, as a group, they are contributing both their explicit and tacit assumptions underlying the Syrian refugee education response. We argue that the foremost goal is wider access, particularly addressing the formal education needs of the 542,000 out-of-school Syrian refugee children in Lebanon, Turkey, and Jordan.

A significant challenge is that many of these goals conflict with each other. In the face of conflicting goals, the education response community risks gridlock in making decisions and moving forward on crucial issues, or of "making the perfect the enemy of the good," as the expression goes. Trade-offs will have to be made; for example, between access and quality, access and integration, or native-language education and host-country language proficiency.

For example, expanding access quickly might by default entail hiring less-experienced teachers, as has been the case, with crowded classrooms. Or, ideally, wider access to education would be rolled out in Jordan and Lebanon, with integration of the Syrians with the Lebanese and Jordanians in single-shift schools, but this may not be possible because of lack of school spaces, host community unwillingness, or Syrian needs. An expedient may be additional double-shifted schools with different children separated from each other, even if this does not meet goals of integration or of equity. If schools are not double-shifted, there will not be enough school spaces in the short run, and without

Table 6.1
Goals for an Access Strategy for Out-of-School Syrian Refugee Children

Goal	Description
Universal access to formal primary education	Involved parties should work to provide access to a formal program of primary education, whether provided by a government, UN program, or alternative program.
Cost-effectiveness	Policymakers should understand the cost implications of various options and make informed choices about which ones best serve a goal of using scarce resources as effectively as possible. Select options that are comparably more cost-effective per child.
Using existing resources	There are more resources in existing school systems than are being used. Make use of existing resources, such as school buildings, Syrian refugees who are teachers, and transportation systems.
Enabling different future scenarios	While no one knows how long most of the Syrians will stay, it should be determined which approaches would best enable two scenarios: one in which the refugees leave soon (ramping down education access programs within a few years), and the other in which this population is served for the longer term.
Host community relations	The large number of refugees understandably causes fears among host communities. Policymakers should aim to reduce, or at least not inflame, host-community tensions through education policies.
Equity	Host communities resent that international assistance goes toward Syrians when they also have vulnerable native populations. Programs should be targeted toward vulnerable communities in an integrated and equitable way.
Shared responsibility	Expenses and planning should be shared by the international community, host countries, and the Syrians themselves.
Political feasibility	Governments face their own pressures and have their own priorities. Options that are optimal from a technical education perspective may face political challenges. It is important to include political considerations in planning and decisionmaking.
Government capacity	Decisions should be based on strengthening government capacity to manage into the future, instead of creating a parallel system of workarounds managed by the international community.
Speed	Approaches that could be scaled up quickly to address out-of-school children within the next year should get first consideration.
Benefits to host countries	Some approaches could benefit the host-country governments and citizens as well as relieve the burdens of the refugees' presence.
Quality and values	A coordinated approach should be taken with the aim of providing refugees with a quality of education that is equal to what host-country children would receive. Educational programming should support national values.

Table 6.1—Continued

Goal	Description
Safety	The school environment and transportation should be safe for children.
Sustainability	Approaches to education should be sustainable. In this case, that means that if the Syrians remain in these countries for the medium to long term, management of education can transition away from the international community to the governments, avoiding another UNRWA-like situation.
Cohesive national identities	Syrian identity should be maintained among refugees so that Syrians can return home. At the same time, maintain cohesive national identities in the host countries, without tensions among people of different nationalities, religions, and ethnicities.
Native language education	The rights of minorities to native-tongue education should be supported, and Syrians should be able to maintain Arabic as a mother tongue.
Host country language proficiency	Syrians should have opportunities to become fluent in host-country languages so that they can participate in education and the labor market.
No parallel education system	Creation of a parallel education system for the Syrians that is run by UN agencies for the coming decades and financed by the international community (as is the case with UNRWA) should be avoided.
Integration	Host-country and Syrian children should be integrated into classrooms, so that the Syrians are not perceived as an alienated class with lower-quality, separate education from citizens.
Decisiveness and action	Children need education. Yet political considerations or conflicting goals may make for hard decisions.
Deliberative strategies	Education policies must be developed in a planned way, rather than becoming path-dependent upon structures set up hastily for the emergency.

a robust set of alternative education programs rolled out, many children would not have access to any formal educational programs at all. Access to separate education in a double shift with hastily hired, inexperienced teachers may be better than remaining at home without any learning opportunities or the protection and community of a school.

While these are examples, there are many trade-offs. The access crisis, in particular, is so great that the international and national education actors should acknowledge the trade-offs and make strategic decisions among them—with sustained medium-term support commitments from international donors.

A Research Agenda in Support of Syrian Refugee Education

This scoping study has pointed up the need for additional research in a number of areas in support of evidence-based decisionmaking, planning, implementation, and evaluation of Syrian refugee education. We propose the following research agenda:

- develop a coordinated, comprehensive access strategy for out-of-school Syrian children, including comparison of options for government and alternative formal education
- conduct a survey and analysis of the barriers to education in each of the three host countries and develop plans to address the primary barriers
- develop a model for alternative educational programming, including criteria for conditions when there should be reliance on the public education system versus creating new programs
- analyze cost-effectiveness per child of various options to expand access
- develop an evidence-based approach to an employment policy for Syrians, balancing host-country concerns regarding unemployment with Syrians' needs to support themselves and their children, ameliorating the need for child labor to contribute to the support of families
- assess the costs and the benefits of Syrian refugee presence in the host countries, and develop approaches to further facilitate the benefits

- compare the curriculum standards of Syria, Turkey, Lebanon, and Jordan, and develop an approach that would enable Syrians to meet requirements of both the Syrian education system and the education system of their host country
- conduct GIS mapping of where Syrian children are in the host countries compared with available school spaces for planning current distribution of students as well as planning needs for new school infrastructure.

Abbreviations

3RP	Regional Refugee and Resilience Plan
AFAD	Disaster and Emergency Management Presidency
EMIS	Education Management Information System
GIS	geographic information system
IDP	internally displaced person
ILO	International Labour Organization
IMC	International Medical Corps
INEE	International Network for Education in Emergencies
MEHE	Ministry of Education and Higher Education (in Lebanon)
MOE	Ministry of Education (in Jordan)
MOI	Ministry of Interior (in Jordan)
MONE	Ministry of National Education (in Turkey)
MOPIC	Ministry of Planning and International Cooperation (in Jordan)
NGO	nongovernmental organization
OCHA	United Nations Office for the Coordination of Humanitarian Affairs
OECD	Organisation for Economic Co-Operation and Development
PPP	public-private partnership
REACH	Renewed Efforts Against Child Hunger

RRP6   Regional Response Plan 6

TIMSS   Trends in International Mathematics and Science Study

UN   United Nations

UNHCR   United Nations High Commissioner for Refugees

UNICEF   United Nations Children's Fund

UNRWA   United Nations Relief and Works Agency for Palestine
          Refugees in the Near East

References

3RP—*See* Regional Refugee and Resilience Plan.

AFAD—*See* Disaster and Emergency Management Presidency.

Albayrak, Aydin, "One Out of 10 people in Gaziantep Is Syrian," *Today's Zaman*, February 16, 2014. As of January 14, 2015:
http://www.todayszaman.com/news-339377-one-out-of-10-people-in-gaziantep-is-syrian.html

Alvdalat, Oman Mohammed, "Jordan: Assume 81% of the Cost of the Hosting Syrian Refugees," *Al-Araby* (in Arabic), January 22, 2015. As of January 28, 2015:
http://www.alaraby.co.uk/economy/c75ce268-99ad-4719-b11d-bc5413a10cd2

Anadolu Agency, "Turkey Spends 4–5 Billion on Syrian Refugees," November 4, 2014. As of March 19, 2015:
http://www.aa.com.tr/en/
economy/414843--turkey-spends-4-5-billion-on-syrian-refugees-minister

Bidinger, Sarah, Aaron Lang, Danielle Hites, Yoana Kuzmova, Elena Noureddine, Susan M. Akram, Lys Runnerstrom, and Timothy Kistner, *Protecting Syrian Refugees: Laws, Policies, and Global Responsibility Sharing*, Boston, Mass.: Boston University School of Law, 2014. As of January 21, 2015:
http://reliefweb.int/report/lebanon/
protecting-syrian-refugees-laws-policies-and-global-responsibility-sharing

Black, Ian, "Patience Running Out in Jordan After Influx of Syrian Refugees," *The Guardian*, December 1, 2014. As of January 28, 2015:
http://www.theguardian.com/world/2014/dec/01/
jordan-syrian-refugees-patience-running-out

Bray, Mark, *Double-Shift Schooling: Design and Operation for Cost-Effectiveness*, 3rd ed., Fundamentals of Educational Planning-90, Paris: UNESCO International Institute for Educational Planning, 2008.

Cagaptay, Soner, and Bilge Menekse, *The Impact of Syria's Refugees on Southern Turkey, Revised and Updated*, Washington D.C.: Washington Institute for Near East Policy, Policy Focus 130, July 2014. As of January 14, 2015:
http://www.washingtoninstitute.org/uploads/Documents/pubs/PolicyFocus130_Cagaptay_Revised3s.pdf

Cemiloglu, Dicle, "Language Policy and National Unity: The Dilemma of the Kurdish Language in Turkey," *College Undergraduate Research Electronic Journal*, 2009. As of January 14, 2015:
http://repository.upenn.edu/curej/97/

Cetingulec, Mehmet, "Syrian Refugees Aggravate Turkey's Unemployment Problem," *Al-Monitor*, July 9, 2014. As of March 19, 2015:
http://www.al-monitor.com/pulse/ru/originals/2014/07/cetingulec-syrian-refugees-turkey-unemployment-illegal-work.html

Chatty, Dawn, *Ensuring Quality Education for Young Refugees from Syria in Turkey, Northern Iraq/Kurdistan Region of Iraq (KRI), Lebanon and Jordan*, Refugees Study Centre, Oxford Department of International Development, University of Oxford, 2015. As of March 19, 2015:
http://www.rsc.ox.ac.uk/research/ensuring-quality-education-for-young-refugees-from-syria

Chermack, Thomas J., Susan A. Lynham, and Wendy E. A. Ruona, "A Review of Scenario Planning Literature," *Futures Research Quarterly*, Summer 2001. As of March 19, 2015:
http://www.thomaschermack.com/Thomas_Chermack_-_Scenario_Planning/Research_files/ReviewofSP.PDF

"Child Marriages Double Among Syrian Refugees in Jordan," Agence France Presse, December 13, 2014. As of January 14, 2015:
http://www.i24news.tv/en/news/international/middle-east/54326-141213-child-marriages-double-among-syria-refugees-in-jordan

Conference des Ministres de l'Education, *Le Programme de Formation Initiale des Maitres et de la Double Vacation an Guinee*, Dakar: des Pays Ayant le Francais en Partage, 2003.

Davis, Rochelle, and Abbie Taylor, *Syrian Refugees in Jordan and Lebanon: A Snapshot from Summer 2013*, Georgetown University, Center for Contemporary Arab Studies and Institute for the Study of International Migration, 2013. As of January 14, 2015:
http://ccas.georgetown.edu/story/1242735967441.html

Dhillon, Navtej, and Tarik Yousef, *Generation in Waiting: The Unfulfilled Promise of Young People in the Middle East*, Washington, D.C.: Brookings Institution Press, 2009.

Dinçer, Osman Bahadır, Vittoria Federici, Elizabeth Ferris, Sema Karaca, Kemal Kirişci, and Elif Özmenek Çarmıklı, *Turkey and Syrian Refugees: The Limits of Hospitality*, Washington, D.C.: Brookings Institution, 2013. As of January 14, 2015:
http://www.brookings.edu/~/media/research/files/reports/2013/11/18%20syria%20turkey%20refugees/turkey%20and%20syrian%20refugees_the%20limits%20of%20hospitality%20(2014).pdf

Disaster and Emergency Management Presidency, *Syrian Refugees in Turkey, 2013: Field Survey Results*, Ankara: Republic of Turkey Prime Ministry, 2013. As of January 20, 2015:
https://www.afad.gov.tr/Dokuman/TR/61-2013123015505-syrian-refugees-in-turkey-2013_print_12.11.2013_eng.pdf

Donnelly, Caitlin, and Joanne Hughes, "Contact, Culture and Context: Evidence from Mixed Faith Schools in Northern Ireland and Israel," *Comparative Education*, Vol. 42, No. 4, 2006, pp. 493–516.

Dorman, Stephanie, *Educational Needs Assessment for Urban Syrian Refugees in Turkey*, YUVA Association, 2014.

Dryden-Peterson, Sarah, *Refugee Education: A Global Review*, Geneva: United Nations High Commissioner for Refugees, 2011. As of January 14, 2015:
http://www.unhcr.org/4fe317589.pdf

Euro-Trends, *Study on Governance Challenges for Education in Fragile Situations: Lebanon Country Report*, European Commission, 2009. As of June 16, 2014:
http://www.ineesite.org/uploads/files/resources/Country_Report_-_Lebanon.pdf

Eurydice Network, *Organisation of the Education System in Turkey: 2009/2010*, Education, Audiovisual and Culture Executive Agency, 2011. As of June 16, 2014:
http://www.etf.europa.eu/webatt.nsf/0/60E61005D5CC5AD1C1257AA3002
5212F/$file/Organization%20of%20the%20education%20system%20in%20
Turkey%202009.2010.pdf

Executive Committee of the High Commissioner's Programme, *Protracted Refugee Situations*, UN High Commissioner for Refugees, EC/54/SC/CRP.14, June 10, 2004.
http://www.unhcr.org/40ed5b384.html

Farrell, J. P., and Ernesto Schiefelbein, "Expanding the Scope of Educational Planning: The Experience of Chile," *Interchange*, Vol. 5, No. 2, 1974, pp. 18–30.

Ferris, Elizabeth, Kemal Kirişci, and Salman Shaikh, *Syrian Crisis: Massive Displacement, Dire Needs and a Shortage of Solutions*, Washington, D.C.: Brookings Institution, September 18, 2013. As of March 19, 2015:
http://www.brookings.edu/~/media/research/files/reports/2013/09/18-syria-ferris-shaikh-kirisci/syrian-crisismassive-displacement-dire-needs-and-shortage-of-solutions-september-18-2013.pdf

Fuller, Bruce, Lucia Dellagnelo, Annelie Strath, Eni Santana Barretto Bastos, Maurício Holanda Maia, Kelma Socorro Lopes de Matos, Adélia Luiza Portela, and Sofia Lerche Vieira, "How to Raise Children's Early Literacy? The Influence of Family, Teacher, and Classroom in Northeast Brazil," *Comparative Education Review*, Vol. 43, No. 1, 1999, pp. 1–35.

Gallagher, Tony, *Education in Divided Societies*, London: Palgrave Macmillan Basingstoke, 2004.

Gaziantep City, website, undated. As of January 14, 2015:
http://gaziantepcity.info/en/home

"Glossary of Education Services," Jordan, Education Sector Working Group, May 29, 2014.

Harvard Field Study Group, *Non-Paper on the International Response to the Syrian Refugee Crisis*, Boston, Mass.: Harvard Kennedy School Belfer Center, 2014. As of January 14, 2015:
http://belfercenter.ksg.harvard.edu/files/Harvard%20Field%20Study%20Jordan%20January%202014%20final.pdf

Hughes, Joanne, "Mediating and Moderating Effects of Inter-Group Contact: Case Studies from Bilingual/Bi-National Schools in Israel," *Journal of Ethnic and Migration Studies*, Vol. 33, No. 3, 2007, pp. 419–437.

———, "Are Separate Schools Divisive? A Case Study from Northern Ireland," *British Educational Research Journal*, Vol. 37, No. 5, 2011, pp. 829–850.

Hughes, Joanne, Andrea Campbell, Miles Hewstone, and Ed Cairns, "What's There to Fear? A Comparative Study of Responses to the Out-Group in Mixed and Segregated Areas of Belfast," *Peace and Change*, Vol. 33, No. 4, 2008, pp. 522–548.

Idiz, Semih, "Turkey's Syrian Refugee Problem Spirals out of Control," *Al-Monitor*, July 20, 2014. As of January 28, 2015:
http://www.al-monitor.com/pulse/originals/2014/07/idiz-turkey-syrian-refugees-local-tension-adana-istanbul.html

ILO—*See* International Labour Organization.

IMC—*See* International Medical Corps.

INEE—*See* International Network for Education in Emergencies.

Internal Displacement Monitoring Centre and Norwegian Refugee Council, *Moving Towards Integration: Overcoming Segregated Education for IDPs—Case Study on Education and Displacement in Georgia*, Geneva, September 2011. As of January 14, 2015:
http://www.internal-displacement.org/assets/publications/2011/201109-moving-towards-integration-thematic-en.pdf

International Crisis Group, *The Rising Costs of Turkey's Syrian Quagmire*, Europe Report No 230, April 30, 2014. As of January 14, 2015:
http://www.crisisgroup.org/en/regions/europe/turkey-cyprus/turkey/230-the-rising-costs-of-turkey-s-syrian-quagmire.aspx

International Labour Organization, *Assessment of the Impact of Syrian Refugees in Lebanon and Their Employment Profile*, Geneva: Regional Office for the Arab States, 2014. As of January 28, 2015:
http://www.ilo.org/wcmsp5/groups/public/---arabstates/---ro-beirut/documents/publication/wcms_240134.pdf

International Medical Corps, *Rapid Needs Assessment of Gaziantep-Based Syrian Refugees: Survey Results*, International Medical Corps and Association for Solidarity with Asylum Seekers and Migrants, 2014a.

———, *Rapid Needs Assessment of Istanbul-Based Syrian Refugees Survey Results, January 2014*, Turkey: International Medical Corps and Association for Solidarity with Asylum Seekers and Migrants, 2014b.

International Network for Education in Emergencies, *Minimum Standards for Education: Preparedness, Response, Recovery*, New York, 2010. As of January 14, 2015:
http://www.ineesite.org/eietrainingmodule/cases/learningistheirfuture/pdf/Minimum_Standards_English_2010.pdf

———, "Mapping the Education Response to the Syrian Crisis," 2014. As of January 14, 2015:
http://s3.amazonaws.com/inee-assets/resources/Mapping_the_Education_Response_to_the_Syrian_Crisis_FINAL.pdf

International Rescue Committee, *Reaching the Breaking Point: An IRC Briefing Note on Syrian Refugees in Lebanon*, rescue.org, 2013. As of January 20, 2015:
http://www.rescue.org/sites/default/files/resource-file/Lebanon%20Policy%20Paper,%20Final%20-%20June%202013.pdf

Jenkins, Brian Michael, *The Dynamics of Syria's Civil War*, Santa Monica, Calif.: RAND Corporation, PE-115-RC, 2014, pp. 3–4. As of September 1, 2014:
http://www.rand.org/pubs/perspectives/PE115.html

"Jordan Needs 72 New Schools to Accommodate Refugee Children—Majali," *Jordan Times*, December 3, 2014. As of January 14, 2015:
http://jordantimes.com/
jordan-needs-72-new-schools-to-accommodate-refugee-children----majali

Kasbar, Toufic, "Syria War, Refugees Add to Lebanon's Economic Crisis," *Al-Monitor*, May 18, 2014. As of January 28, 2015:
http://www.al-monitor.com/pulse/politics/2014/05/lebanon-syria-conflict-refugees-economy-challenges-state.html

Kayaoğlu, Barin, "Turkey Restricts Academic Research on Syrian Refugees," *Al-Monitor*, May 27, 2015. As of July 24, 2015:
http://www.al-monitor.com/pulse/originals/2015/05/turkey-syria-government-restricts-academic-research.html

Kirişci, Kemal, *Syrian Refugees and Turkey's Challenges: Going Beyond Hospitality*, Washington, D.C.: Brookings Institution, 2014. As of January 14, 2015:
http://www.brookings.edu/~/media/research/files/reports/2014/05/12%20turkey%20syrian%20refugees%20kirisci/syrian%20refugees%20and%20turkeys%20challenges%20may%2014%202014.pdf

Kirk, Jackie, ed. *Certification Counts: Recognizing the Learning Attainments of Displaced and Refugee Students*, Paris: UNESCO-IIEP, 2009.

Kolcu, Gamze, "350,000 School-Aged Syrian Children in Turkey, Just Half Receiving Education," *Hurriyet Daily News*, October 25, 2014. As of January 14, 2015:
http://www.hurriyetdailynews.com/350000-school-aged-syrian-children-in-turkey-just-half-receiving-education.aspx?PageID=238&NID=73456&NewsCatID=341

Lebanese Institute for Democracy and Human Rights, *The Legal Report of the Situation of the Syrian Refugees in Lebanon*, Beirut, 2013. As of January 21, 2015:
http://www.dchrs.org/english/File/Reports/Syrian_Refugees_in_Lebanon_En.pdf

Linden, Toby, *Double-Shift Secondary Schools: Possibilities and Issues*, Washington, D.C.: World Bank, 2001. As of January 26, 2015:
http://siteresources.worldbank.org/EDUCATION/Resources/278200-1099079877269/547664-1099079967208/Double_shift_secondary_schools_En01.pdf

Loescher, Gil, and James Milner, "Protracted Displacement: Understanding the Challenge," *Forced Migration Review*, No. 33, 2009, pp. 9–11. As of January 14, 2015:
http://www.fmreview.org/en/FMRpdfs/FMR33/FMR33.pdf

MEHE—See Ministry of Education and Higher Education.

Mekki, Najwa, "For Syrian Children in Turkey, School Brings Choices and Challenges," June 10, 2013. As of July 24, 2015:
http://www.unicef.org/education/Turkey_69603.html

Ministry of Education, data shared with authors, Jordan, August 26, 2014.

Ministry of Education and Higher Education, "MEHE Response to the Syrian Crisis," presentation to authors, Lebanon, February 2014a.

———, *Reaching All Children with Education in Lebanon*, June 2014b.

Ministry of Planning and International Cooperation, *Final Draft National Resilience Plan 2014–2016*, Jordan, 2014a. As of January 28, 2015:
http://static1.squarespace.com/static/522c2552e4b0d3c39ccd1e00/t/
53f300ffe4b082b86e9e72bd/1408434431620/NRP_FinalDraft_June2014.pdf

———, *Jordan Response Plan Refugee Pillar Needs Assessment*, Jordan, 2014b.

———, *Jordan Response Plan for the Syria Crisis: 2015*, 2015. As of January 28, 2015:
https://docs.unocha.org/sites/dms/Syria/Jordan%20Response%20Plan.pdf

MOE—*See* Ministry of Education.

MOPIC—*See* Ministry of Planning and International Cooperation.

Morand, MaryBeth, Katherine Mahoney, Shaula Bellour, and Janice Rabkin, *The Implementation of UNHCR's Policy on Refugee Protection and Solutions in Urban Areas: Global Survey—2012*, Geneva: UN High Commissioner for Refugees, 2013. As of January 2015:
http://www.unhcr.org/516d658c9.pdf

Naylor, Hugh, "Syrian Refugees Become Less Welcome in Lebanon, as New Entry Rules Take Effect," *Washington Post*, January 5, 2015. As of January 28, 2015:
http://www.washingtonpost.com/world/syrian-refugees-become-less-welcome-in-lebanon-as-new entry-rules-take-effect/2015/01/05/7e412f59-b357-4af4-95a4-5edf3df7af06_story.html

Nebehay, Stephanie, "Syrians Largest Refugee Group After Palestinians: U.N.," January 7, 2015. As of January 15, 2015:
http://www.reuters.com/article/2015/01/07/
us-mideast-crisis-syria-refugees-idUSKBN0KG0AZ20150107

Niens, Ulrike, and Ed Cairns, "Conflict, Contact, and Education in Northern Ireland," *Theory into Practice*, Vol. 44, No. 4, 2005, pp. 337–344.

OCHA—*See* United Nations Office for the Coordination of Humanitarian Affairs.

OECD—*See* Organisation for Economic Co-Operation and Development.

Olwan, Mohamed Y., *Iraqi Refugees in Jordan: Legal Perspective*, CARIM Analytic and Synthetic Notes 2009/22, Legal Module, 2009. As of January 14, 2015:
http://cadmus.eui.eu/handle/1814/11253

Organisation for Economic Co-Operation and Development, *Education at a Glance 2009: OECD Indicators*, Paris, 2009. As of July 24, 2015:
http://www.oecd.org/edu/skills-beyond-school/
educationataglance2009oecdindicators.htm

Orhan, Oytun, *The Situation of Syrian Refugees in the Neighboring Countries: Findings, Conclusions, and Recommendations*, Ankara: Center for Middle Eastern Strategic Studies (ORSAM), Report No: 189, April 2014. As of January 14, 2015: http://www.orsam.org.tr/en/enUploads/Article/Files/201452_189ing.pdf

Ouseley, Herman, *Community Pride Not Prejudice: Making Diversity Work in Bradford*, Bradford, UK: Bradford Vision, 2001.

Özer, Serap, Selçuk Şirin, and Brit Oppedal, *Bahçeşehir Study of Syrian Refugee Children in Turkey*, 2013. As of January 21, 2015: http://www.fhi.no/dokumenter/4a7c5c4de3.pdf

Parkinson, Sarah E., *Educational Aftershocks for Syrian Refugees in Lebanon*, Washington, D.C.: Middle East Research and Information Project, September 7, 2014. As of January 14, 2015: http://www.merip.org/educational-aftershocks-syrian-refugees-lebanon

PeaceGeeks, "UNHCR App for Syrian Refugees," undated. As of January 20, 2015: http://digitalhumanitarians.com/content/unhcr-app-syrian-refugees

Pettigrew, Thomas F., and Linda R. Tropp, "A Meta-Analytic Test of Intergroup Contact Theory," *Journal of Personality and Social Psychology*, Vol. 90, No. 5, May 2006, pp. 751–783.

"Prince El-Hassan: Syrian Refugees Crisis Requires National-Level Thinking," Ammon News, December 7, 2014. As of January 20, 2015: http://en.ammonnews.net/article.aspx?articleno=27251#.VJlCqV4BA

Pryor, Michael, "New Model Partnership," *Public Private Finance*, May 2006, pp. 17–19. As of January 2015: http://connection.ebscohost.com/c/articles/20904654/new-model-partnership

REACH—See Renewed Efforts Against Child Hunger.

Regional Refugee and Resilience Plan, *3RP Regional Progress Report, June 2015*, 2015a. As of September 22, 2015: http://www.3rpsyriacrisis.org/wp-content/uploads/2015/06/3RP-Progress-Report.pdf

———, *Regional Quarterly Update—March 2015: Education*, 3RP Regional Refugee & Resilience Plan 2015–2016, 2015b. As of January 28, 2015: http://www.3rpsyriacrisis.org/

———, *Regional Refugee and Resilience Plan 2015–2016 in Response to the Syria Crisis: Regional Strategic Overview*, 2015c. As of January 28, 2015: http://www.3rpsyriacrisis.org/wp-content/uploads/2015/01/3RP-Report-Overview.pdf

———, *Regional Refugee and Resilience Plan 2015–2016: Lebanon*, 2015d. As of January 28, 2015:
http://www.3rpsyriacrisis.org/wp-content/uploads/2014/12/3RP-Report-Lebanon-formatted.pdf

———, *Regional Refugee and Resilience Plan 2015–2016: Turkey*, 2015e. As of January 28, 2015:
http://www.3rpsyriacrisis.org/wp-content/uploads/2015/01/3RP-Report-Turkey-A4-low-res.pdf

Renewed Efforts Against Child Hunger, *Access to Education for Syrian Refugee Children in Zaatari Camp, Jordan—Joint Education Needs Assessment Report*, Jordan: Education Sector Working Group, 2014a. As of July 24, 2015:
https://data.unhcr.org/syrianrefugees/download.php?id=7394

———, *Akkar Public Schools Assessment: Akkar District—North Governorate—Lebanon: Assessment Report March 2014*, Geneva: United Nations High Commissioner for Refugees, 2014b.

———, *Joint Education Needs Assesment Report: Access to Education for Syrian Refugee Children and Youth in Host Communities*, Jordan: Education Sector Working Group, 2015. As of July 24, 2015:
https://data.unhcr.org/syrianrefugees/download.php?id=8570

Rotberg, Robert I., *Corruption, Global Security, and World Order*, Washington, D.C.: Brookings Institution Press, 2009.

"Schools Pilot Launched," *Middle East Economic Digest (MEED)*, December 15, 2006.

Shteiwi, Musa, Jonathan Walsh, and Christina Klassen, *Coping with the Crisis: A Review of the Response to Syrian Refugees in Jordan*, Center for Strategic Studies, 2014. As of January 26, 2015:
http://www.jcss.org/Photos/635520970736179906.pdf

Sinclair, Margaret, "Education in Emergencies," in Jeff Crisp, Christopher Talbot, and Daiana B. Cipollone, eds., *Learning for a Future: Refugee Education in Developing Countries*, Geneva: United Nations High Commissioner for Refugees, 2001. As of March 19, 2015:
http://www.unhcr.org/cgi-bin/texis/vtx/home/opendocPDFViewer.html?docid=4a1d5ba36&query=Education%20in%20Emergencies

Song, Suzan, *Mental Health/Psychosocial and Child Protection Assessment for Syrian Refugee Adolescents in Za'atari Refugee Camp, Jordan*, Amman: UN Children's Fund, International Medical Corps, 2013. As of January 21, 2015:
http://reliefweb.int/report/jordan/mental-healthpsychosocial-and-child-protection-assessment-syrian-refugee-adolescents

Stainback, John, and Michael B. Donahue, "Outside the Budget Box—Public/ Private Partnership as a Creative Vehicle for Finance and Delivery of Public School Facilities," *Journal of Professional Issues in Engineering Education and Practice*, Vol. 131, No. 4, 2005, pp. 292–296.

"Syrian Refugees Get to Work in Turkey," *Al-Monitor*, July 22, 2014. As of January 2015:
http://www.al-monitor.com/pulse/politics/2014/07/syrian-refugees-turkey-provide-work.html

TIMSS—*See* Trends in International Mathematics and Science Study.

Trends in International Mathematics and Science Study, "TIMSS (Trends in International Mathematics and Science Study) 2011," 2012. As of January 21, 2015:
http://timssandpirls.bc.edu/data-release-2011/pdf/Overview-TIMSS-and-PIRLS-2011-Achievement.pdf

UNHCR—*See* United Nations High Commissioner for Refugees.

UNICEF—*See* United Nations Children's Fund.

United Nations, *Universal Declaration of Human Rights*, December 10, 1948. As of October 14, 2015:
http://www.un.org/en/documents/udhr/index.shtml

———, *Convention Relating to the Status of Refugees*, July 28, 1950. As of October 14, 2015:
http://www.ohchr.org/EN/ProfessionalInterest/Pages/StatusOfRefugees.aspx

———, *Convention on the Rights of the Child (61st plenary meeting ed.)*, New York, United Nations General Assembly, A/RES/44/25, 1989. As of October 14, 2015:
http://www.ohchr.org/en/professionalinterest/pages/crc.aspx

———, *The Right to Education of Migrants, Refugees and Asylum- Seekers, Report of the Special Rapporteur on the Right to Education, Vernor Muñoz*, New York, United Nations General Assembly, A/HRC/14/25, April 16, 2010a. As of October 15, 2015:
http://www2.ohchr.org/english/bodies/hrcouncil/docs/14session/A.HRC.14.25_en.pdf

———, *The Right to Education in Emergency Situations: Resolution*, New York, United Nations General Assembly, A/RES/64/290, July 27, 2010b. As of October 15, 2015:
http://www.refworld.org/docid/4c6241bb2.html

United Nations Children's Fund, *Shattered Lives: Challenges and Priorities for Syrian Children and Women in Jordan*, Amman, Jordan, June 2013a. As of July 2014:
http://www.unicef.org/infobycountry/files/Shattered_Lives_June10.pdf

———, *A Lost Generation? A Strategy for Children Affected by the Syrian Crisis,* October 2013b. As of January 14, 2015:
http://www.unicef.org/appeals/files/Lost_Generation_-_Final_Draft_for_distribution_to_participants_09Oct2013.pdf

———, *No Lost Generation: Protecting the Futures of Children Affected by the Crisis in Syria, Strategic Overview,* 2014a. As of July 2014:
http://childrenofsyria.info/wp-content/uploads/2014/01/No-Lost-Generation-Strategic-Overview-January-2014-RV.pdf

———, *A Study on Early Marriage in Jordan 2014,* Amman, 2014b. As of January 21, 2015:
http://www.unicef.org/mena/UNICEFJordan_EarlyMarriageStudy2014.pdf

United Nations Education, Scientific and Cultural Organization, *Jordan—UNESCO: Country Programming Document (UCPD) 2012–2017,* Amman, 2012. As of January 14, 2015:
http://unesdoc.unesco.org/images/0021/002166/216664e.pdf

United Nations High Commissioner for Refugees, "UNHCR Country Operations Plan 2004—Lebanon," 2003. As of January 21, 2015:
http://www.refworld.org/docid/3fd9c6a14.html

———, "UNHCR Policy on Refugee Protection and Solutions in Urban Areas," Geneva, September 2009. As of January 14, 2015:
http://www.unhcr.org/cgi-bin/texis/vtx/home/opendocPDFViewer.html?docid=4ab356ab6&query=UNHCR Policy on Refugee Protection and Solutions in Urban Areas

———, *Ensuring Access to Education: Operational Guidance on Refugee Protection and Solutions in Urban Areas,* Geneva, 2011a. As of January 14, 2015:
http://www.unhcr.org/4ea9552f9.html

———, *2012–2016 Education Strategy,* Geneva, 2012. As of January 14, 2015:
http://www.unhcr.org/5149ba349.html

———, *The Future of Syria: Refugee Children in Crisis,* November 2013. As of September 2014:
http://reliefweb.int/sites/reliefweb.int/files/resources/Future-of-Syria-UNHCR-v13.pdf

———, *2014 Syria Regional Response Plan, Strategic Overview: Mid-Year Update,* 2014a. As of January 14, 2015:
http://www.unhcr.org/syriarrp6/midyear/docs/syria-rrp6-myu-strategic-overview.pdf

———, *Inter-Agency Multi-Sector Needs Assessment (MSNA) Phase One Report: Secondary Data Review and Analysis (May 2014),* 2014b. As of January 14, 2015:
http://data.unhcr.org/syrianrefugees/download.php?id=6241

———, *Mental Health and Psychosocial Well-Being of Children*, 2014c. As of January 21, 2015:
http://www.refworld.org/docid/540ef77c4.html

———, "UNHCR Global Trends 2013: War's Human Cost," 2014d. As of January 14, 2015:
http://www.unhcr.org/5399a14f9.html

———, "Regional: RRP6 Monthly Update—March 2014 (Education)," 2014e. As of January 20, 2015:
http://data.unhcr.org/syrianrefugees/download.php?id=7289

———, *Syrian Refugees Living Outside Camps in Jordan*, March 18, 2014f. As of January 14, 2015:
http://reliefweb.int/report/jordan/syrian-refugees-living-outside-camps-jordan

———, data shared with authors, July 11, 2014g.

———, "Jordan Inter-Agency Operational Update," September–October 2014h. As of November 2014:
http://www.unhcr.org/5465c15d9.html

———, "2015 UNHCR Country Operations Profile—Syrian Arab Republic," 2015a. As of November 2015:
http://www.unhcr.org/pages/49e486a76.html

———, "2015 UNHCR Country Operations Profile—Turkey," 2015b. As of January 2015:
http://www.unhcr.org/pages/49e48e0fa7f.html

———, *UNHCR Global Trends: Forced Displacement in 2014*, Geneva, 2015c. As of July 24, 2015:
http://unhcr.org/556725e69.html#_ga=1.225701913.2095888809.1417795315

———, "Syria Regional Refugee Response: Regional Overview," September 22, 2015d. As of September 22, 2015:
http://data.unhcr.org/syrianrefugees/regional.php

United Nations Office for the Coordination of Humanitarian Affairs, *Syria Humanitarian Bulletin, Issue 1*, June 5, 2012. As of March 19, 2015:
http://reliefweb.int/sites/reliefweb.int/files/resources/Full_doc_37.pdf

———, *Syria Humanitarian Bulletin, Issue 18*, January 2013a.

———, *Syria Humanitarian Bulletin, Issue 29*, July 2013b.

———, *Syria Humanitarian Bulletin, Issue 40*, January 2014a.

———, *Syria Humanitarian Bulletin, Issue 49*, July 2014b.

———, *Syria Humanitarian Bulletin, Issue 52*, January 2015.

United Nations Relief and Works Agency for Palestine Refugees in the Near East, "Education in Lebanon," 2013. As of January 14, 2015:
http://www.unrwa.org/activity/education-lebanon

UNRWA—*See* United Nations Relief and Works Agency for Palestine Refugees in the Near East.

Van Laar, Colette, Shana Levin, and Jim Sidanius, "Ingroup and Outgroup Contact: A Longitudinal Study of the Effects of Cross-Ethnic Friendships, Dates, Roommate Relationships and Participation in Segregated Organizations," in Wagner, Ulrich, Linda R. Tropp, Gillian Finchilescu, and Colin Tredoux, eds., *Improving Intergroup Relations: On the Legacy of Thomas F. Pettigrew*, Oxford, UK: Blackwell, 2008, pp. 127–142.

World Bank, "Education Reform for Knowledge Economy I Program: Overview," undated. As of January 21, 2015:
http://www.worldbank.org/projects/P075829/
education-reform-knowledge-economy-program?lang=en

———, *Lebanon: Economic and Social Impact Assessment of the Syrian Conflict*, Report No. 81098-LB, September 2013. As of March 19, 2015:
http://www-wds.worldbank.org/external/default/WDSContentServer/WDSP/IB/
2013/09/24/000333037_20130924111238/Rendered/PDF/
810980LB0box379831B00P14754500PUBLIC0.pdf

———, "Population, Total," 2015. As of January 28, 2015:
http://data.worldbank.org/indicator/SP.POP.TOTL

Yeginsu, Ceylan, "Turkey Strengthens Rights of Syrian Refugees," *New York Times*, December 29, 2014. As of January 14, 2015:
http://www.nytimes.com/2014/12/30/world/europe/turkey-strengthens-rights-of-
syrian-refugees.html?partner=rss&emc=rss&smid=tw-nytimesworld&_r=1

Yukhananov, Anna, "World Bank OKs $150 Mln to Help Jordan with Syria Refugees," Reuters, July 18, 2013. As of January 14, 2015:
http://www.reuters.com/article/2013/07/18/
syria-crisis-worldbank-idUSL1N0FO1YY20130718